JERRY SILVERMAN'S FOLK GUITAR METHOD

GROSSET & DUNLAP

Publishers   New York

Photographs pages iii and 1 by C. F. Martin
Organization, Nazareth, Pennsylvania.
Photographs on pages 2, 3, and 131 by Gaynor.

Library of Congress catalog card number: 73-22733
ISBN 0-448-11641-3
Published simultaneously in Canada
First printing

Printed in the United States of America

CONTENTS

JERRY SILVERMAN'S FOLK GUITAR METHOD

1

CHORDS and NOTES

We are going to approach the guitar from two directions simultaneously. Chords will be illustrated by the simple diagram method and notes will be taught based upon the songs being sung. By this chord-note integrated method you will very quickly be able to read melodies of unfamiliar songs as well as enlarge your chord vocabulary and right hand technique.

The Anatomy of the Guitar

There are two types of guitars which are well-suited for vocal accompaniment. They are the nylon-string (classical) guitar and the steel-string (acoustic) guitar. The difference between these two instruments, apart from some physical considerations, is the tone or timbre they produce when played. Many beginners favor the nylon-string guitar. In either case, care

must be taken to obtain the best instrument possible to assure ease of fingering, accuracy of pitch and beauty of tone.

The Anatomy of the Guitarist

The fingernails of your left hand must be as short as possible. This cannot be stressed too vigorously—especially for the beginner. The fingernails of your right hand should be left a little longer, with some white showing. They should be rounded off, never pointed.

The left hand supports the neck of the guitar. The left thumb presses against the back of the neck for support. The remaining fingers of the left hand press down the strings to play individual notes or groups of notes (chords).

The right hand strums or plucks the strings in various ways. Right-hand technique will be a major area of discussion throughout this book.

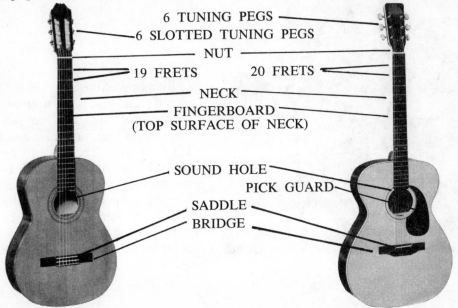

6 TUNING PEGS
6 SLOTTED TUNING PEGS
NUT
19 FRETS   20 FRETS
NECK
FINGERBOARD
(TOP SURFACE OF NECK)

SOUND HOLE
PICK GUARD
SADDLE
BRIDGE

You may either stand or sit while playing the guitar during a performance. For your studies, the seated position is recommended.

The Capo

You need one additional piece of equipment: a **capo**. This is a small elastic clamp that fits over all the strings at particular positions on the neck of the guitar. It will be absolutely indispensable to you as you begin to sing your way through this book. Its use will be explained shortly.

The Open Strings and the Chord Diagram

The guitar has six strings tuned to six different notes. The thinnest string is the first string. It has the highest pitch. As the diameter of each neighboring string increases, the pitch gets lower. The sixth string is the thickest. It has the lowest pitch.

Let's take a closer look at the strings near the nut.

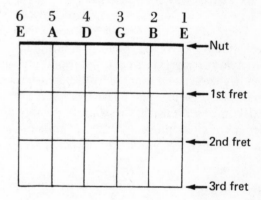

By means of this diagram we can now clearly identify the strings by note and number. But even more important, we can now use this diagram to indicate where the fingers of your left hand should be placed to play chords. As stated before, the left thumb is placed behind the neck as a counterpressure to the fingers. The index finger is the first finger. The fingers after it are numbered 2, 3, and 4, respectively.

In playing the following E minor chord, press with your fingertips as close to the second fret as possible without actually touching it. The strings should be brought into firm contact with that fret. Any loosening of pressure will result in an unclear, muffled sound. Also, be careful not to touch any other string with your palm or fingers.

Strum down across all six strings with your right thumb.

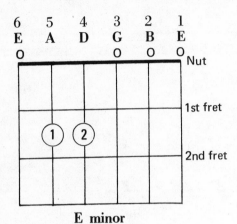

E minor

- A circle (o) over an open (unfingered) string tells you to play that string also.

- Thumb on 6th string
- 1st fingertip on underside of 3rd string
- 2nd fingertip on underside of 2nd string
- 3rd fingertip on underside of 1st string

If any string does not give you a clear note see if you can find out why not. Don't grip the neck of the guitar too tightly. There should be "daylight" between your palm and the neck. Your fingertips will soon begin to develop slight callouses. This will help to give you better sounding notes.

The Basic Right-Hand Strum

Let your right arm rest at about the elbow on the side of the guitar with your hand hanging down limply. Your hand should be over the sound hole. Notice how the fingers curve slightly inward. Move only the hand toward the strings so that the fingers and thumb make contact with the strings as follows:

The thumb strikes the sixth string. *Don't bend the thumb!* Keep it relatively stiff and move it in a circular orbit away from the sixth string and then back again to it for the next beat.

The three fingers, which are resting lightly on the underside of their respective strings move inward toward the palm in a gentle plucking action. *Don't move the wrist or the arm!* Just pluck the strings lightly.

Alternate between a thumb beat and a finger beat. Move slowly and evenly at a comfortable "walking pace."

"Thumb-fingers, thumb-fingers . . . one-two, one-two . . . bass chord, bass chord . . ."

To play your first song (and all other songs) start playing the chord slowly before you start singing. When you sing follow the "guitar rhythm" above the music: T = thumb, F = fingers.

3

Hey Ho, Nobody Home

Note Reading

Music is written on a five-line staff. The notes may be written either on the lines or in the spaces between the lines. Each line and space represents a particular note and has a letter of the alphabet from A to G assigned to it. After G we start all over again from A.

The symbol called the **G clef** is written at the beginning of each staff of guitar music. It serves to fix specific note names to the lines and spaces of the staff. (There are other clefs used for other instruments which give the lines and spaces other note names.)

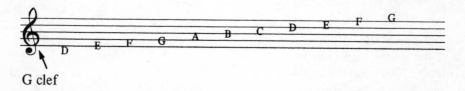

G clef

The notes on the staff are all playable on the guitar. Before we go on to playing our first ex- ercise, however, there are a few other items that must be mentioned.

The **quarter note,** ♩, is the basic unit of time. By itself, it does not indicate how fast it is to be played. Once the determination of speed has been made (by the composer, conductor or performer) it is usually the quarter note which is counted, as in "one-two-three-four . . ." We say that the quarter note gets "the beat."

A piece of music is usually divided into segments, or **measures,** having the same number of beats and separated from each other by **bar lines.**

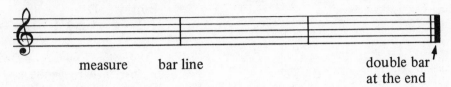

measure   bar line   double bar
                                                        at the end

The **time signature** written at the beginning of the piece tells us how many beats are in each measure. If there are four quarter-note beats per measure the time signature is $\frac{4}{4}$ (four-quarter time, or simply, four-four).

The purpose of the **key signature,** written directly after the G clef, will become apparent as you go along through this book. Suffice it to say, at present, that it alters the position of certain notes on the guitar. The key signature of *Hey Ho, Nobody Home* is F sharp. (Because F is the top line of the staff, that's where the sharp is written, but it affects all other F's —high and low.)

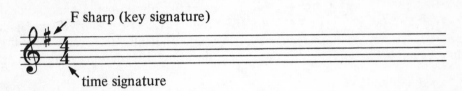

F sharp (key signature)

time signature

To find the actual notes on the guitar from the music, the following number system has been used: The first numeral indicates the string and the second numeral indicates the fret. For example, **4/2 = 4th string, 2nd fret; 3/0 = 3rd string, open (unfingered).**

The fingering for the right hand is given as "T" for thumb, with "1" and "2" indicating first and second fingers.

For the left hand use the fingers which correspond to the number of the fret (1st finger, 1st fret, etc.).

Try to maintain a slow, steady, *even* count of "1-2-3-4" for the quarter notes in this simplified version of *Hey Ho, Nobody Home.*

Here, once again, are the seven notes that make up the melody of *Hey Ho, Nobody Home.* Get to know them by name as well as position on the guitar.

Most songs need more than one chord for their accompaniment. The E minor chord is often coupled with the D major chord.

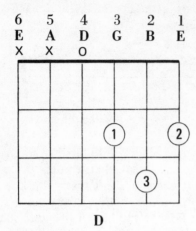

6 5 4 3 2 1
E A D G B E
X X O

D

• An x over an open string tells you not to play that string.

Notice how the first and second fingers move from E minor to D.

For the D chord the thumb strikes the fourth (D) string. The fingers pluck up on the first three strings as before.

Practice switching back and forth from Em to D:

Em   D   Em
1-2-3-4   1-2-3-4   1-2-3-4 etc.

What Shall We Do with the Drunken Sailor? has been written here in the key of E minor. However, it may be too high for some people to sing in that key. Here is where your capo comes in. The capo, when put in place across all the strings at any fret, raises the pitch of all the strings by the same amount. You then finger your chords as before, but place them to the right of the capo (as you hold your guitar). The capo takes the place of the nut.

You will probably be able to sing this song comfortably with the capo "on" the third or fourth fret (that is, right up against but not quite touching the fret). The first note will then be 2/0 (counting from the capo).

What Shall We Do with the Drunken Sailor?

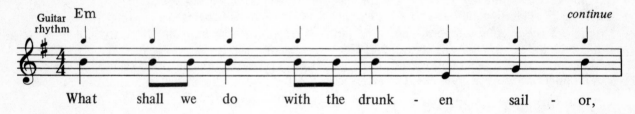

What shall we do with the drunk - en sail - or,

What shall we do with the drunk-en sail - or, What shall we do with the

drunk - en sail - or, Ear - lye in the morn - ing?

6

Em
Chorus Way hey, and up she rises,
D
Way hey, and up she rises,
Em
Way hey, and up she rises,
D   Em
Earlye in the morning.

Em
Put him in the long boat till he's sober,
D
Put him in the long boat till he's sober,
Em
Put him in the long boat till he's sober,
D   Em
Earlye in the morning. *Chorus*

Em
Put him in the scuppers with a hose pipe on him,
D
Put him in the scuppers with a hose pipe on him,
Em
Put him in the scuppers with a hose pipe on him,
D   Em
Earlye in the morning. *Chorus*

Em
Heave him by the leg in a running bowline,
D
Heave him by the leg in a running bowline,
Em
Heave him by the leg in a running bowline,
D   Em
Earlye in the morning. *Chorus*

Em
That's what we'll do with the drunken sailor,
D
That's what we'll do with the drunken sailor,
Em
That's what we'll do with the drunken sailor,
D   Em
Earlye in the morning. *Chorus*

Note Reading

Here is a rhythmically simplified version of *What Shall We Do with the Drunken Sailor?* Of the nine different notes which make up the melody six have already been found in *Hey Ho, Nobody Home.*

Rhythmically, there is one new element: the **half note.**

If the quarter note gets one count (one beat), the half note gets two. It is not played twice—it is held for the total time of two beats.

Right hand

Here are the nine notes which make up the melody of *What Shall We Do with the Drunken*

Sailor? Get to know them by name and position.

The Key of D Major

The feeling of **key** is established by, among other things, the beginning and ending chords. In most folk songs these two chords are the same. So, if a song begins with a D chord it will generally end with a D chord. When this happens we say that the song is in the key of D.

The D chord is said to be the **tonic chord** of the key of D. It is also called the **I chord** (Roman numerals are used to indicate types of chords). The most important other chord in a major key is the chord beginning on the fifth note of the scale.

D E F♯ G A
1 2 3   4 5

The fifth note of the D scale is A. The chord built on the fifth note (V) is called the **dominant chord.** We often add "something" to this dominant chord, changing it into a **dominant seventh** (V7). The V7 of D is A7.

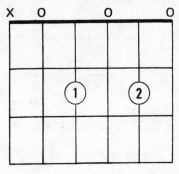

A7

Notice how the first and second fingers move from D to A7.

For the A7 chord the thumb strikes the fifth (A) string. The fingers pluck the first three strings as before.

Practice switching back and forth from D to A7.

D   A7   D
1-2-3-4   1-2-3-4   1-2-3-4 etc.

Keep your capo handy in case *Skip to My Lou* doesn't suit your vocal range in D.

Skip to My Lou

Skip, skip, skip to my lou, Skip, skip, skip to my lou,

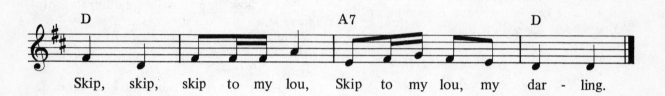

Skip, skip, skip to my lou, Skip to my lou, my dar - ling.

D
Lost my partner, what'll I do?
A7
Lost my partner, what'll I do?
D
Lost my partner, what'll I do?
A7   D
Skip to my Lou, my darling. *Chorus*

D
Little red wagon painted blue,
A7
Little red wagon painted blue,
D
Little red wagon painted blue,
A7   D
Skip to my Lou, my darling. *Chorus*

D
I'll get another one prettier than you,
A7
I'll get another one prettier than you,
D
I'll get another one prettier than you,
A7   D
Skip to my Lou, my darling. *Chorus*

D
Flies in the buttermilk, shoo fly, shoo,
A7
Flies in the buttermilk, shoo fly, shoo,
D
Flies in the buttermilk, shoo fly, shoo,
A7   D
Skip to my Lou, my darling. *Chorus*

D
Gone again, skip to my Lou,
A7
Gone again, skip to my Lou,
D
Gone again, skip to my Lou,
A7   D
Skip to my Lou, my darling. *Chorus*

Note Reading

You have already learned five of the six different notes which make up the melody of *Skip to My Lou*.

Rhythmically, there is one new element: **eighth notes.** Eighth notes may be written individually

or tied together in groups of two or more.

Two eighth notes take the time of one quarter note. In a melody containing quarter notes and eighth notes we count "one-and-two-and" to give us the relative timing of the eighth notes.

two beats per measure

Count: 1   2   1   2   1   2 and 1 and 2 and 1 and 2

Here is a simplified version of *Skip to My Lou.*

F sharp   D   A   E   C sharp   G
4/4   4/0   3/2   4/2   5/4   3/0
Count: 1   2   1   2   *continue*

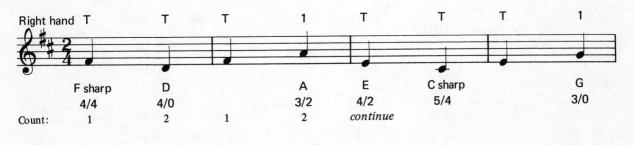

Count: 1   2 - and   1   2

Here are the six notes which make up the melody of *Skip to My Lou*. Do you know them all?

C sharp   D   E   F sharp   G   A
5/4   4/0   4/2   4/4   3/0   3/2

11

Pay Me My Money Down

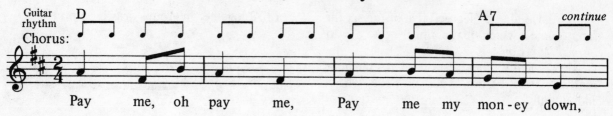

Pay me, oh pay me, Pay me my mon-ey down,

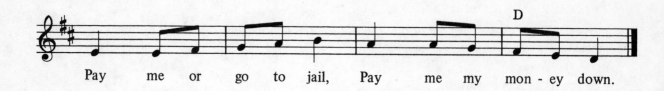

Pay me or go to jail, Pay me my mon-ey down.

D
Thought I heard the captain say,
    A7
    Pay me my money down,

"Tomorrow is our sailing day."
    D
    Pay me my money down. *Chorus*

D
Next day we cleared the bar,
    A7
    Pay me my money down,

He knocked me down with the end of a spar,
    D
    Pay me my money down. *Chorus*

D
Wish I was Mister Howard's son,
    A7
    Pay me my money down,

Sit in the house and drink good rum,
    D
    Pay me my money down. *Chorus*

D
Wish I was Mister Steven's son,
    A7
    Pay me my money down,

Go to town and have some fun,
    D
    Pay me my money down. *Chorus*

Note Reading

There are no new notes in the melody of
Pay Me My Money Down.

Pay attention to the eighth notes.

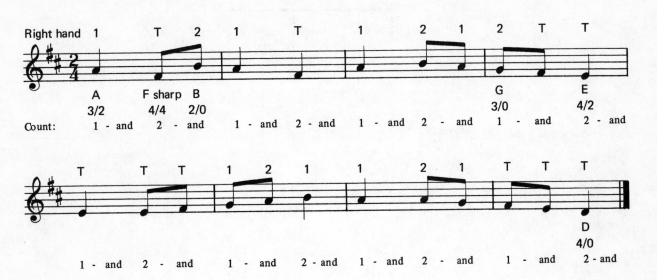

Here are the six notes which make up the
melody.

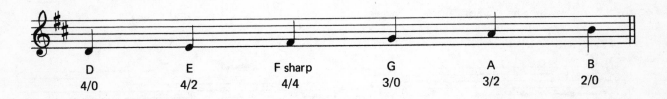

If we add two more notes to this group we
get a **D major scale.** The key signature of D
major is two sharps: F sharp and C sharp.

D Major Scale

13

The G major chord is often found in combination with E minor as well as with D chords. In the key of E minor, G is the **III chord.** E minor is also called the **relative minor** of G major.

Notice that the first finger does not move when you switch back and forth between E minor and G. The thumb plays the sixth string for both chords.

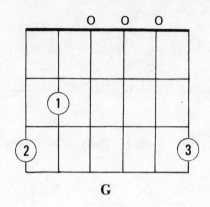

G

The Butcher Boy

Guitar rhythm

Em — She went up-stairs _____ to— make her bed, _____

G — And not a word _____ to her moth-er said. _____

— Her moth-er she _____ went up-stairs too, _____

G — Say-ing,"Daugh-ter, oh daugh-ter, _____ what— trou-bles you?"

14

Em
"Oh mother, oh mother, I cannot tell,
       G   Em
That butcher boy I love so well.

He courted me my life away,
       G   Em
And now at home he will not stay.

Em
"There is a place in London Town,
       G   Em
To where he goes and sits him down.

He takes that strange girl on his knee,
       G   Em
And tells her what he won't tell me."

Em
Her father, he came home from work,
         G   Em
Saying, "Where is daughter, she seems so hurt?"

He went upstairs to give her hope,
       G   Em
And found her hanging from a rope.

Em
He took his knife and cut her down,
       G   Em
And in her bosom these words he found:

"Go dig my grave both wide and deep,
       G   Em
Place a marble slab at my head and feet.

And over my coffin place a snow-white dove,
       G   Em
To warn the world I died of love."

Alternate Bass

Some of you must be wondering why you need to finger the fifth and fourth strings for E minor and the fifth string for G if you never play those strings with your right hand. Actually, those other strings should be played. Your thumb can alternate from sixth to fifth string (or to fourth) for E minor. Try it. . . . The same alternate bass can be played with G. Be careful not to muffle the fifth string with the second finger.

By the way, the alternate bass for the D chord is the fifth string and for the A7 either the sixth or the fourth strings.

Note Reading

There are no new notes in the melody of *The Butcher Boy,* but there are four new musical symbols.

- The **quarter-note rest** ⌡ is a period of silence equivalent in time to a quarter note. Here it pertains to the vocal part, not to the guitar, which plays throughout.

- The **whole note** ○ gets four beats. It is played once and held for the equivalent of four quarter notes.

- The **tie** 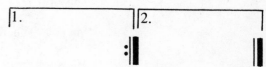 joins two or more notes of the same pitch across a bar line. The result is a note which is played once but is held for the total time of the notes tied together. In *The Butcher Boy,* we have a whole note tied to a quarter note, giving us a note which is held for five beats.

- **Repeat signs** ‖: :‖ indicate that the musical passage between them should be repeated. Often these signs are coupled with first and second endings.

The first time the passage is played you play the music under the first ending up to the repeat sign. For the repeat you skip the music under the first ending and go directly to the second ending.

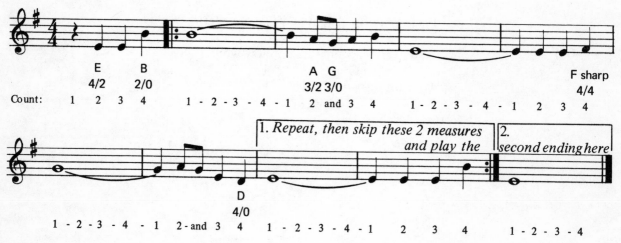

16

If we add one more note we get an **E minor scale.** The key signature of E minor is F sharp.

E Minor Scale (Natural Minor)

E	F sharp	G	A	B	C	D	E
4/2	4/4	3/0	3/2	2/0	2/1	2/3	1/0
					new note		

As mentioned before, the G chord is often played in the key of D. It is the chord built on the fourth note of the D major scale. The **IV chord** is also called the **subdominant.**

D, G and A7 are the three most important chords in the key of D. As you learn to play in other keys you will see that the chords whose relationships to those keys is this same I, IV and V will be the mainstays of those keys as well.

17

When the Saints Go Marching In

Oh, when the saints _____ go march-ing in, _____

Count: 1 2 3 4 | 1 - 2 - 3 - 4 - 1 | 2 3 4 | 1 - 2 - 3 - 4 -

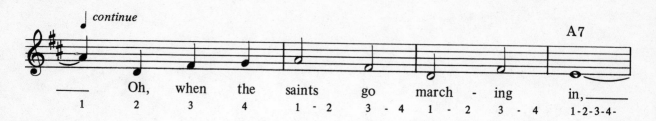

_____ Oh, when the saints go march - ing in, _____

1 2 3 4 | 1 - 2 3 - 4 1 - 2 3 - 4 | 1-2-3-4-

_____ Oh Lord, I want to be in that num - ber _____

1 2 3 4 | 1 - 2 - 3 4 | 1 - 2 3 4 | 1 2-3-4-

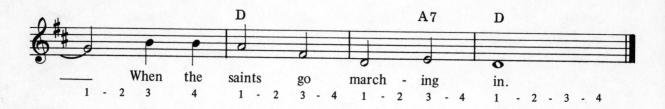

_____ When the saints go march - ing in.

1 - 2 3 4 | 1 - 2 3 - 4 | 1 - 2 3 - 4 | 1 - 2 - 3 - 4

D
And when the sun refuse to shine,
                                       A7
And when the sun refuse to shine.
                   D   G
Oh Lord, I want to be in that number,
               D   A7 D
When the sun refuse to shine.

18

D
And when the moon drips red with blood,
         A7
And when the moon drips red with blood.
     D   G
Oh Lord, I want to be in that number,
     D   A7 D
When the moon drips red with blood.

D
And when the trumpet sounds a call,
         A7
And when the trumpet sounds a call.
     D   G
Oh Lord, I want to be in that number,
     D   A7 D
When the trumpet sounds a call.

D
And when the revelation comes,
        A7
And when the revelation comes.
     D   G
Oh Lord, I want to be in that number,
    D A7 D
When the revelation comes.

Repeat first verse

Note Reading

There are no new notes in the melody but there is one new musical symbol: the **dotted half note** .

$$\text{♩.}$$

A dot after a note increases that note's time value by one half its original value. A dot after a half note, therefore, adds a quarter note in time to the half note. The new note is then equal to three quarter notes total time. It gets three beats.

Go back and play the melody of *When the Saints Go Marching In,* paying strict attention to the rests, ties, dots and right-hand fingering (thumb on the fourth string, first and second fingers alternating on the third string).

In the key of D, the E minor chord is the **II chord**. It appears much less frequently than the G(IV) and A7 (V7) chords. Its function is often to lead into the V7 which then resolves to I. This II—V7—I sequence is an important **chord progression.**

Blow, Ye Winds, in the Morning

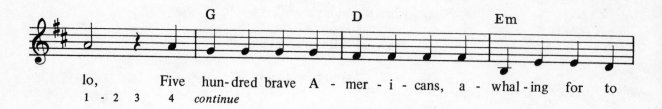

'Tis ad - ver - tised in Bos - ton, New York and Buf - fa -

Count: 4 1 2 3 4 1 2 3 4 1 2 3 4

lo, Five hun-dred brave A - mer - i - cans, a - whal-ing for to

1 - 2 3 4 *continue*

go. _____ Sing - ing, Blow, ye winds in the morn - ing, And

1 2 3 4 - and

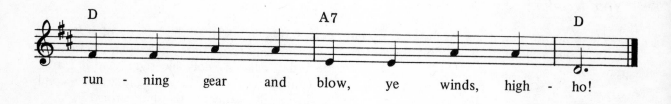

blow ye winds high - ho. Clear a - way the

run - ning gear and blow, ye winds, high - ho!

D
They'll send you to New Bedford

That famous whaling port,
G   D
And give you to some land-sharks there,
Em   A7
To board and fit you out. *Chorus*

D
They'll tell you of the clipper-ships,

A-going in and out;
G   D
And say you'll take five hundred sperm
Em   A7
Before you're six months out. *Chorus*

D
It's now we're out to sea, my boys,

The wind begins to blow.
G   D
One half the watch is sick on deck,
Em   A7
The other half below. *Chorus*

D
The skipper's on the quarter-deck,

A-squinting at the sails,
G   D
When up aloft the lookout cries,
Em   A7
"There goes a school of whales!" *Chorus*

D
Now, clear away the boats, my boys,

And after him we'll travel.
G   D
But if you get too near his fluke,
Em   A7
He'll kick you to the devil. *Chorus*

D
It's now we've got him all turned up,

We tow him alongside.
G   D
We over with our blubber hooks,
   Em   A7
And rob him of his hide. *Chorus*

D
Next comes the stowing down, my boys,

'Twill take both night and day.
G   D
You'll all have fifty cents apiece,
Em   A7
When you draw your pay. *Chorus*

D
When we get home, our ship made fast,

And we get through our sailing,
G   D
A winding glass around we'll pass,
Em   A7
And damn this blubber whaling. *Chorus*

Note Reading

There is one new note in the melody of *Blow, Ye Winds in the Morning*.

A
5/0

Continued→

There are also three new musical symbols.

slur

- The **slur** indicates that one syllable is sung on two or more different notes.

- The **light double bar** separates sections of a piece of music, as for example, verse and chorus.

- The **half-note rest** is a period of silence equivalent in time to a half note. Here it is two beats of vocal silence.

Also observe that the first note of this song comes before the first complete measure of four quarter notes. It is called an **upbeat.** In a sense it is the fourth beat of the preceding measure. When you sing the song make sure that you sing the first note on an up-pluck and not a thumb beat. This will insure that the first beat of the first complete measure gets its customary thumb beat and that you will be "in step" for the rest of the song.

When a song begins with an upbeat it is customary practice to reduce the number of beats in the last measure by the amount taken by the upbeat. Hence, the last measure here has only three beats. Look back at *When the Saints Go Marching In.* There the song begins with three upbeats so the last measure has only one quarter note.

Now, go back and play *Blow, Ye Winds in the Morning,* watching out for eighths, quarters, halfs, dotted halfs, rests and right-hand fingering.

Three-Quarter (¾) Time

When a song has three beats per measure it is said to be in **three-quarter time.** The time signature is written ¾. As far as the guitar is concerned the basic thumb-finger-pluck is extended by one more finger-pluck. The feeling is now *"one-two-three . . . one-two-three . . . thumb-fingers-fingers . . . thumb-fingers-fingers. . . ."*

Practice this new strum with your old chords *. . . bass-chord-chord . . . one-two-three . . . thumb-fingers-fingers.*

Observe that *Pretty Saro,* which is in three-quarter time, begins on an upbeat. That means you start singing on the third beat of your strum. This will insure that the first word, "in," of the first complete three-beat measure will get a thumb beat.

Pretty Saro

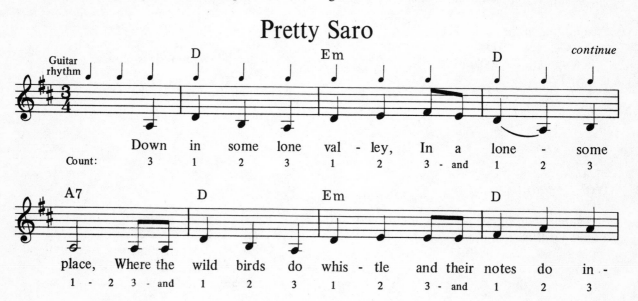

crease, Fare - well, ___ Pret - ty Sa - ro, I ___ bid you a -
1 - 2　3　1　2　3 - and　1　2　3 - and　1　2　3

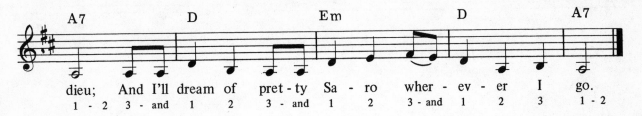

dieu; And I'll dream of pret - ty Sa - ro wher - ev - er I go.
1 - 2　3 - and　1　2　3 - and　1　2　3 - and　1　2　3　1 - 2

D　　　Em　　D　　A7
My love she won't have me, so I understand.
D　　　Em　　　D
She wants a freeholder who owns house
　　A7
　　and land.
D　　G　　　D　　A7
I cannot maintain her with silver and gold,
D　　Em　　　　D
And all of the fine things that a big house
　　A7
　　should hold.

D　　　Em　　　　　D
If I were a merchant and could write a
　　　A7
　　fine hand,
D　　Em　　D　　A7
I'd write her a letter that she'd understand.
D　　　G　　　　D
I'd write her by the river, where the waters
　　A7
　　do flow,
D　　　　Em　　D　A7
And I'll dream of pretty Saro wherever I go.

Note Reading

The five notes that make up the melody of *Pretty Saro* form a **pentatonic scale:**

Pentatonic songs do not always have the same chord progressions as songs based upon major scales. Even though *Pretty Saro* is harmonized with chords that seem to suggest **D** major, you will observe that the melody begins and ends on the note A and that the final chord is not D, but A7.

There is no new rhythmic or note material in *Pretty Saro*. You should be able to play it without too much difficulty.

23

The Streets of Laredo begins on the third beat of the strum.

The Streets of Laredo

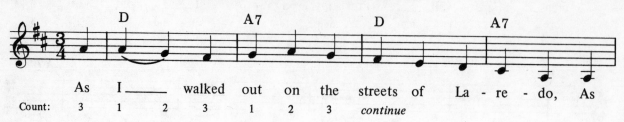

As I____ walked out on the streets of La - re - do, As

Count: 3   1   2   3   1   2   3   *continue*

I walked out in La - re - do one day, I

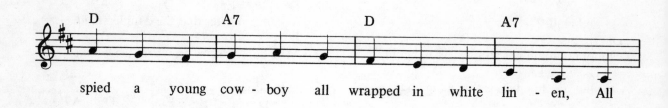

spied a young cow - boy all wrapped in white lin - en, All

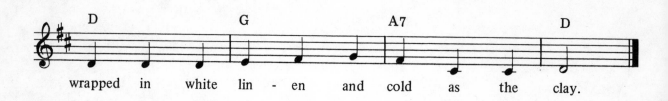

wrapped in white lin - en and cold as the clay.

| | D | A7 | D | A7 |
"I see by your outfit that you are a cowboy,"
| | D | G | D | A7 |
These words he did say, as I boldly walked by;
| | D | A7 | D | A7 |
"Come sit down beside me and hear my sad story,
| | D | G | A7 | D |
I'm shot in the breast and I know I must die.

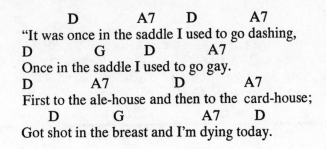

<pre>
    D   A7   D   A7
"It was once in the saddle I used to go dashing,
D   G   D   A7
Once in the saddle I used to go gay.
D   A7   D   A7
First to the ale-house and then to the card-house;
    D   G   A7   D
Got shot in the breast and I'm dying today.

    D   A7   D   A7
"Get sixteen gamblers to handle my coffin,
    D   G   D   A7
And six jolly cowboys to sing me a song.
    D   A7   D   A7
Take me to the graveyard and lay the sod o'er me,
    D   G   A7   D
For I'm a young cowboy and I know I've done wrong.

    D   A7   D   A7
"Oh, beat the drum slowly and play the fife lowly,
    D   G   D   A7
And play the dead march as you carry me along.
    D   A7   D   A7
Put bunches of roses all over my coffin,
    D   G   A7   D
For I'm a young cowboy and I know I've done wrong."
</pre>

Repeat first verse

Note Reading

There are no new problems here. Just watch
out for C sharp; we haven't seen it since *Skip
to My Lou.*

The Key of G Major

The three main chords in the key of G—the I, IV and V7 chords—are G, C, and D7. You may want to revise your fingering of the G chord in order to facilitate changing to C. It is not unusual for a chord to have different fingerings depending upon what other chords are being played with it.

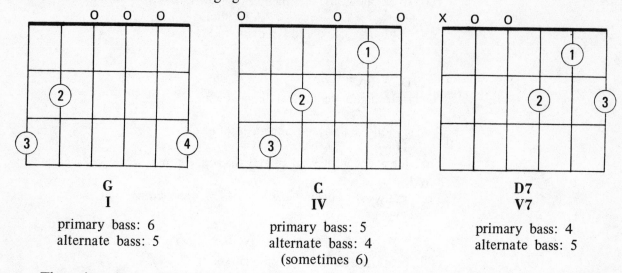

G
I

primary bass: 6
alternate bass: 5

C
IV

primary bass: 5
alternate bass: 4
(sometimes 6)

D7
V7

primary bass: 4
alternate bass: 5

The guitar rhythm for *Greenland Fisheries* is your basic strum played as eighth notes. All that means is that for every quarter note of melody you play one complete bass-chord cycle. Since the song starts with an upbeat of two eighth notes you sing the first word, " 'twas," on a thumb beat on the G chord and the second word, "in," on an up-pluck.

Greenland Fisheries

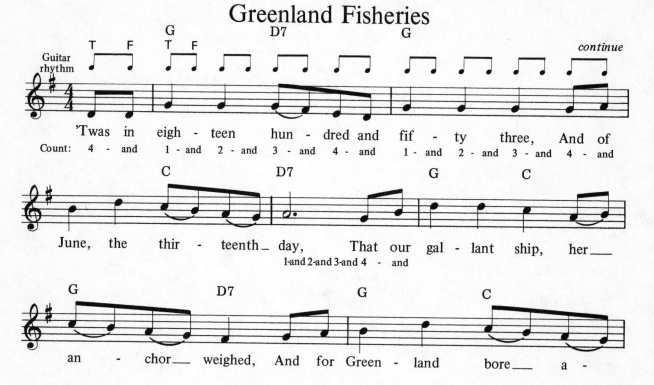

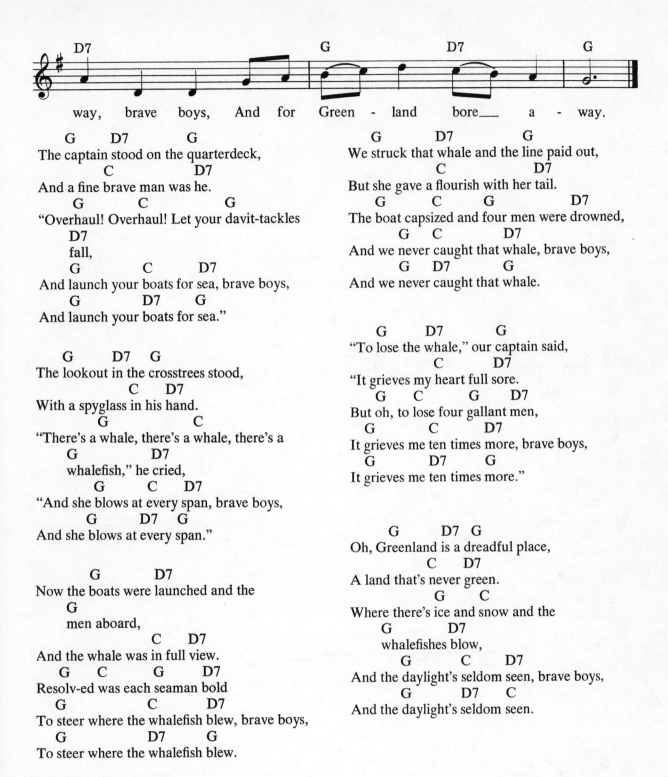

way,   brave   boys,   And   for   Green - land   bore___ a - way.

      G   D7   G
The captain stood on the quarterdeck,
           C   D7
And a fine brave man was he.
      G   C   G
"Overhaul! Overhaul! Let your davit-tackles
      D7
      fall,
      G   C   D7
And launch your boats for sea, brave boys,
      G   D7   G
And launch your boats for sea."

       G   D7 G
The lookout in the crosstrees stood,
             C D7
With a spyglass in his hand.
        G   C
"There's a whale, there's a whale, there's a
       G   D7
       whalefish," he cried,
         G   C   D7
"And she blows at every span, brave boys,
         G   D7 G
And she blows at every span."

         G   D7
Now the boats were launched and the
      G
      men aboard,
             C   D7
And the whale was in full view.
      G   C   G   D7
Resolv-ed was each seaman bold
      G   C   D7
To steer where the whalefish blew, brave boys,
      G   D7   G
To steer where the whalefish blew.

       G   D7   G
We struck that whale and the line paid out,
             C   D7
But she gave a flourish with her tail.
      G   C   G   D7
The boat capsized and four men were drowned,
        G   C   D7
And we never caught that whale, brave boys,
        G D7   G
And we never caught that whale.

         G   D7   G
"To lose the whale," our captain said,
              C   D7
"It grieves my heart full sore.
      G   C   G   D7
But oh, to lose four gallant men,
      G   C   D7
It grieves me ten times more, brave boys,
      G   D7   G
It grieves me ten times more."

        G   D7 G
Oh, Greenland is a dreadful place,
            C   D7
A land that's never green.
          G   C
Where there's ice and snow and the
        G   D7
       whalefishes blow,
         G   C   D7
And the daylight's seldom seen, brave boys,
      G   D7   C
And the daylight's seldom seen.

Note Reading

There is one note that we have not had in any song so far.

C

2/1

27

Gee, but I Wanna Go Home

The cof - fee that they give you, They say is might - y fine, It's

Count: and 1 - and 2 - and 3 - and 4 - and 1 - and 2 - and 3 - and 4 - and

good for cuts and bruis - es, And it tastes like i - o - dine.

continue

Chorus:

I don't want no more of ar - my life,

1 - and - 2 - and

Gee, but I wan - na go home. _____

1 - and 2 and 3 - and 4 - and 1 - and - 2 - and - 3 - and - 4

G
The biscuits that they give you, they
    D7
    say are mighty fine,
                                    G
One rolled off a table and it killed a pal

    of mine. *Chorus*

G
The chickens that they give you, they
    D7
    say are mighty fine,
                              G
One rolled off the table and it started

    marking time. *Chorus*

G
The women in the service club, they
    D7
    say are mighty fine,
                                  G
But most are over ninety and the rest are

    under nine. *Chorus*

G
The details that they give you, they
    D7
    say are mighty fine,
                                    G
The garbage that we pick up they feed

    us all the time. *Chorus*

G
The clothing that they give you, they
    D7
    say is mighty fine,
                                G
But me and my buddy can both fit into

    mine. *Chorus*

G   D7
They treat us all like monkeys and make

    us stand in line,
                              G
They give us fifty dollars and take back

    forty-nine. *Chorus*

Note Reading

The dotted quarter note ♩. gets the equivalent of three eighths in total time. Since the accompaniment is an eighth-note strum, each dotted quarter gets three beats—that is, *bass-chord-bass . . . one-and-two,* or *three-and-four,* depending upon where in the measure it appears.

When playing the melody, watch out also for the eighths—quarter—eighths sequence in the first measure. Make sure you count it properly.

I Ride an Old Paint

I ride an old paint, ___ I lead an old dan, ___ I'm

Count: 3 1-and-2 and 3-and 1 2 3 1-and-2 and 3-and *continue*

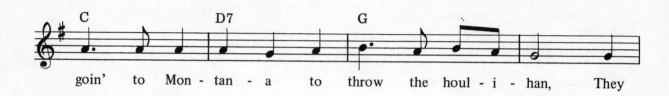

goin' to Mon - tan - a to throw the houl - i - han, They

feed in the cou - lies, They wa - ter in the draw, Their

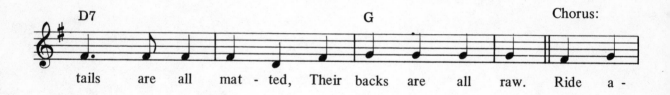

tails are all mat - ted, Their backs are all raw. Ride a -

Chorus:

round, lit - tle do - gies, Ride a - round ___ them slow, For the

fi - ery and snuf - fy are rar - ing to go.

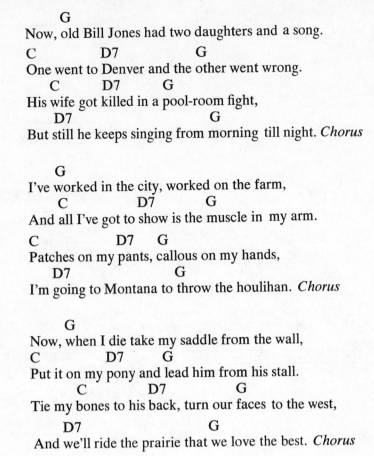

     G
Now, old Bill Jones had two daughters and a song.
C   D7   G
One went to Denver and the other went wrong.
    C   D7   G
His wife got killed in a pool-room fight,
    D7   G
But still he keeps singing from morning till night. *Chorus*

     G
I've worked in the city, worked on the farm,
     C   D7   G
And all I've got to show is the muscle in my arm.
C   D7   G
Patches on my pants, callous on my hands,
    D7   G
I'm going to Montana to throw the houlihan. *Chorus*

     G
Now, when I die take my saddle from the wall,
C   D7   G
Put it on my pony and lead him from his stall.
    C   D7   G
Tie my bones to his back, turn our faces to the west,
    D7   G
And we'll ride the prairie that we love the best. *Chorus*

Note Reading

There is no new material in *I Ride an Old Paint*. Just watch out for the dotted quarters within the three-beat measures.

Finger E minor this way—it works better
with your new G fingering.

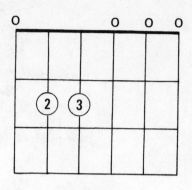

E minor

primary bass: 6
alternate bass: 5, 4

The Gypsy Rover

The gyp - sy ro - ver come o - ver the hill,
Count: and 1 2 3 4 - and 1 2 - and 3 - 4

Bound   through the val - ley so shad - y;   He
continue

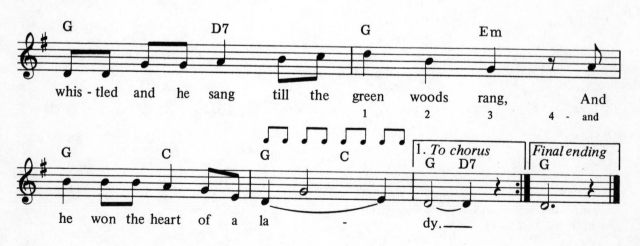

whis - tled and he sang   till   the   green   woods   rang,   And
1   2   3   4 - and

he won the heart of a la - dy.

Chorus (same music as verse)

G   D7   G   D7
Ah di do, ah di do da day,
G   C   G D7
Ah di do, ah di day dee.
    G   D7   G   Em
He whistled and he sang till the green woods rang,
    G   C   G CG (D7)
And he won the heart of a la-a-a-dy. *last time no D7*

G   D7 G   D7
She left her father's castle gate,
G   C   G D7
She left her own true lover.
   G   D7   G Em
She left her servants and her estate,
G   C   G C G D7
To follow the gypsy ro-o-o-ver. *Chorus*

   G   D7   G   D7
Her father saddled his fastest steed,
G   C   G D7
Roamed the valley all over.
 G   D7   G   Em
Sought his daughter at great speed,
    G   C   G C G D7
And the whistling gypsy ro-o-o-ver. *Chorus*

G   D7   G   D7
He came at last to a mansion fine,
G   C   G D7
Down by the River Claydie.
    G   D7   G   Em
And there was music and there was wine,
    G   C   G C.G D7
For the gypsy and his la-a-a-dy. *Chorus*

G   D7   G   D7
"He's no gypsy, my father," said she,
    G   C   G D7
"My lord of freelands all over,
    G   D7   G   Em
And I will stay till my dying day
     G   C   G C G D7
With my whistling gypsy ro-o-o-ver." *Chorus*

Note Reading

There are no new notes here. There is one new musical symbol: **eighth-note rest** ♪. It represents a period of silence equivalent in time to one eighth note.

To play G major scales in the lower and middle **octaves** we need to learn four new notes. From these scales we see that the key signature of G major is F sharp—the same as for E minor, which is the **relative minor** of G major. The relative minor has the same key signature as its **relative major**. To find the relative minor of any major key, count six notes up from the first note of the scale. (E is the sixth note of the scale of G.)

G Major Scale (Lower Octave)

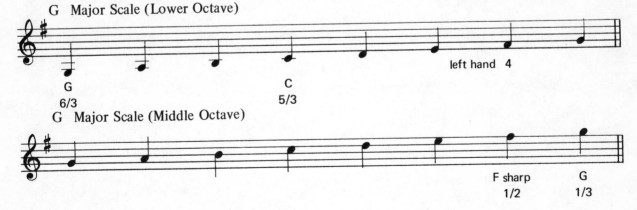

left hand 4

G
6/3

C
5/3

G Major Scale (Middle Octave)

F sharp
1/2

G
1/3

33

The Key of A Major

The three main chords in the key of A major —the I, IV and V7 chords—are A, D and E7. There are at least two possible fingerings for the A chord. One involves covering the fourth and third strings with the first finger. Another uses three different fingers for the three notes. Which do you find more comfortable?

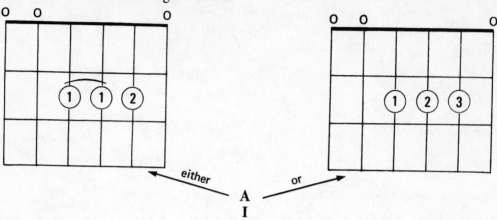

A
I

primary bass: 5
alternate bass: 6, 4

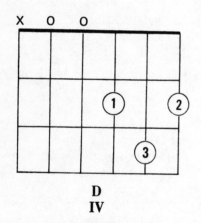

D
IV

primary bass: 4
alternate bass: 5

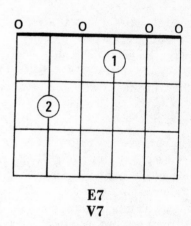

E7
V7

primary bass: 6
alternate bass: 5
(sometimes 4)

Bring a Little Water, Sylvie

continue

Guitar rhythm
Chorus:

Bring a lit - tle wa - ter, Syl - vie,

Bring a lit - tle wa - ter, now.

Bring a lit - tle wa - ter, Syl - vie

Ev - 'ry lit - tle once in a while.

A
Don't you see me coming?
E7
Don't you see me now?
A   D
Don't you see me coming,
        A
Ev'ry little once in a while?   *Chorus*

A
Don't you hear me coming?
E7
Don't you hear me now?
A   D
Don't you hear me coming,
            A
Every little once in a while?   *Chorus*

A
Bring it in a bucket, Sylvie.
E7
Bring it in a bucket now.
A   D
Bring it in a bucket, Sylvie.
        A
Ev'ry little once in a while.   *Chorus*

Note Reading

There are no new notes in *Sylvie,* but there is one interesting point. With the exception of the D-chord section (measures 6 and 7) all the notes of the melody are to be found in the chords A and E7. That means that if you play the chords properly you should be able to play the melody without moving your left hand except to change chords. (This will work also with the D chord when the melody note is A.)

35

Brennan on the Moor

continue

'Tis __ of a brave young high-way-man this sto-ry I will tell, His name was Wil-lie Bren-nan and in Ire-land he did dwell. It was on the Kil-wood Moun-tain he com-menced his wild ca-reer. And man-y a weal-thy no-ble-man be-fore him shook with fear.

Chorus:

It was Bren-nan on the moor, Bren-nan on the moor, Bold __ brave and un-daunt-ed was young Bren-nan on the moor.

A
One day upon the highway,
D   A
As Willie, he went down,

He met the mayor of Cashiell
                    E7
A mile outside the town.
     A
The mayor knew his features,

And he said, "Young man," said he,
       D
"Your name is Willie Brennan,
          A
You must come along with me."   *Chorus*

     A
Now, Brennan's wife had gone to town,
D   A
Provisions for to buy.

And when she saw her Willie,
                    E7
She commenced to weep and cry.
     A
Said, "Hand to me that tenpenny."

As soon as Willie spoke,
   D
She handed him a blunderbuss
     A
From underneath her cloak.   *Chorus*

A
Now, with this loaded blunderbuss,
D   A
The truth I will unfold,

He made the mayor tremble
                    E7
And he robbed him of his gold.
     A
One hundred pounds was offered

For his apprehension there.
       D
And he, with horse and saddle,
          A
To the mountains did repair.   *Chorus*

A
Now, Brennan, being an outlaw,
D   A
Upon the mountains high,

With cavalry and infantry
                    E7
To take him they did try.
     A
He laughed at them so scornfully,

Until at last, 'twas said,
       D
That by a woman false of heart
          A
He cruelly was betrayed.   *Chorus*

Note Reading

There is no new material here. Just watch
out for the eighth note and dotted quarter note
passages in the chorus.

The Four Marys

Last night there were____ four Ma - rys, This

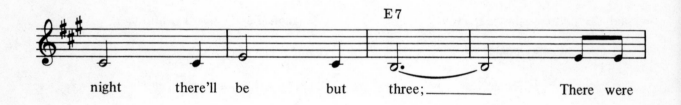

night there'll be but three;____ There were

Ma - ry Bea - ton and Ma - ry Sea - ton and

Ma - ry Car - mi - chael and me.____

      A   D   A
Oh, often have I dressed my queen,
                 E7
And put on her braw silk gown.
   A   D   A D
But all the thanks I've got tonight,
      A   E7   A
Is to be hanged in Edinburgh Town.

      A   D   A
Full often have I dressed my queen,
               E7
Put gold upon her hair.
   A   D   A
But I have got for my reward
  A   E7   A
The gallows to be my share.

      A   D   A
Oh, little did my mother know,
                 E7
The day she cradled me,
      A   D   A   D
The land I was to travel in,
     A   E7   A
The death I was to dee.

      A   D A
Oh, happy, happy is the maid
                  E7
That's born of beauty free.
      A   D   A   D
It was my rosy dimpled cheeks
     A   E7   A
That's been the death of me.

          A   D   A
They'll tie a kerchief around my eyes,
               E7
That I may not see to dee.
       A   D   A   D
And all they'll tell my parents dear
     A   E7   A
Is that I'm across the sea.

Repeat verse one

Note Reading

There is one new note here.

G sharp
3/1

Revolutionary Tea

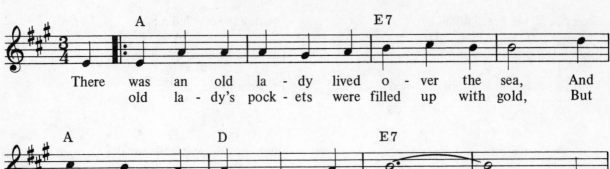

There was an old la - dy lived o - ver the sea, And
old la - dy's pock - ets were filled up with gold, But

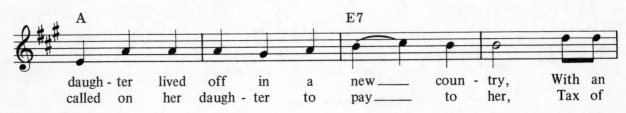

she was an is - land queen._____ Her
nev - er con - tent - ed, she._____ She

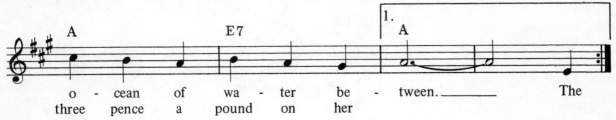

daugh - ter lived off in a new_____ coun - try, With an
called on her daugh - ter to pay_____ to her, Tax of

o - cean of wa - ter be - tween._____ The
three pence a pound on her

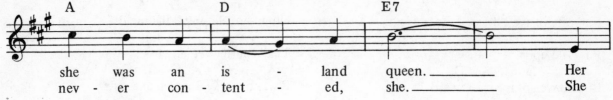

tea, of three pence a pound on her tea._____

A   E7
"Now mother, dear mother," the daughter
   replied,
A   D   E7
"I sha'n't do the thing that you ax.
A   E7
I'm willing to pay a fair price for the tea,
A   E7   A
But never a threepenny tax."

"You shall!" quoth the mother, and
   E7
   reddened with rage,
               D   E7
"For you're my own daughter, you see.
A   E7
And sure, 'tis quite proper the daughter
   should pay
A   E7   A
Her mother a tax on the tea,
D   A   E7   A
Her mother a tax on the tea."

```
        A              E7
And so the old lady her servant called up,
        A         D        E7
And packed off a budget of tea.
        A                  E7
And eager for three pence a pound, she put in
A        E7        A
Enough for a large family.

                          E7
        She ordered her servant to bring home
            the tax,
        A         D        E7
        Declaring her child should obey,
          A              E7
        Or old as she was and a woman most
            grown,
            A         E7   A
        She'd half whip her life away,
        D    A        E7   A
        She'd half whip her life away.
```

```
        A                        E7
The tea was conveyed to the daughter's door,
        A         D    E7
All down by the oceanside.
          A                    E7
But the bouncing girl poured out every last
            pound
          A         E7        A
In the dark and the boiling tide.

                                E7
        And then she called out to the Island
            Queen,
            A         D        E7
        "Oh mother, dear mother," quoth she,
            A                    E7
        "Your tea you may have when it is steeped
            enough,
            A    E7        A
        But never a tax from me,
        D    A    E7        A
        But never a tax from me."
```

Note Reading

No new material here but watch out for the repeat and the different first and second endings. If this song is too high for you don't forget your capo.

The key signature of A major is three sharps:

F sharp, C sharp and G sharp. We know all the notes needed to play the A major scale in its lower octave. For the middle octave we need to learn two new notes.

A Major Scale (Lower Octave)

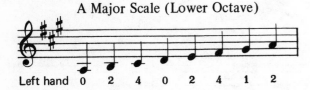

Left hand   0   2   4   0   2   4   1   2

A Major Scale (Middle Octave)

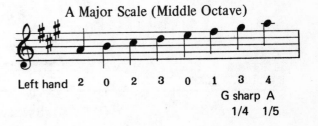

Left hand   2   0   2   3   0   1   3   4
                                G sharp A
                                1/4   1/5

41

The Key of E Major

The three main chords in the key of E major
—the I, IV and V7 chords—are E, A and B7.

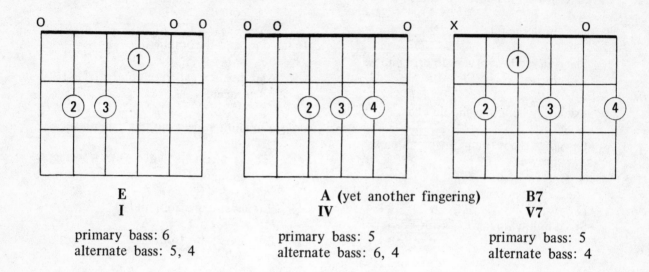

E
I

A (yet another fingering)
IV

B7
V7

primary bass: 6
alternate bass: 5, 4

primary bass: 5
alternate bass: 6, 4

primary bass: 5
alternate bass: 4

You may have to put your capo on the second fret if this song is too low for you.

Good News

char - i - ot's a - com - in', And I don't want it to leave a - me be -

hind. Get up in the char - i - ot, car - ry me home, Get

up in the char - i - ot, car - ry me home, Get up in the char - i - ot,

car - ry me home, Don't want it to leave me be - hind.

E
There's a long white robe in Heaven, I know,
B7   **E**
A long white robe in Heaven, I know.

There's a long white robe in Heaven, I know,
     A   **B7**   **E**
Don't want it to leave me behind.   *Chorus*

E
There's a better land in this world, I know,
B7   **E**
A better land in this world, I know.

There's a better land in this world, I know,
     A   **B7**   **E**
Don't want it to leave me behind.   *Chorus*

         E
There's peace and freedom in this world, I know,

B7   **E**
Peace and freedom in this world, I know.

There's peace and freedom in this world, I know,
       A   **B7**   **E**
Don't want it to leave me behind.   *Chorus*

Note Reading

Three new notes on the sixth string.

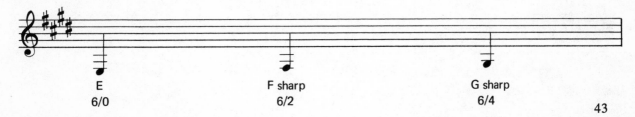

     E   F sharp   G sharp
    6/0   6/2   6/4

Crawdad

You get a line and I'll get a pole, — hon - ey, ————

You get a line and I'll get a pole, — ba - by, ————

You get a line and I'll get a pole and we'll go fish - ing by the

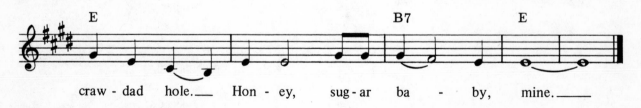

craw - dad hole. — Hon - ey, sug - ar ba - by, mine. —

E
Get up, old man, you slept too late, honey.
                              B7
Get up, old man, you slept too late, baby.
      E
Get up, old man, you slept too late,
A   E
Last piece of crawdad's on your plate
              B7   E
   Honey, sugar baby, mine.

E
Along come a man with a sack on his back,
   honey.

Along come a man with a sack on his back,
   B7
   baby.
E
Along come a man with a sack on his back,
A   E
Packing all the crawdads he can pack,
              B7   E
   Honey, sugar baby, mine.

      E
Get up, old woman, you slept too late, honey.
                                 B7
Get up, old woman, you slept too late, baby.
      E
Get up, old woman, you slept too late,
A   E
Crawdad man done passed your gate,
              B7   E
   Honey, sugar baby, mine.

E
What you gonna do when the lake goes dry,
   honey?

What you gonna do when the lake goes dry,
   B7
   baby?
E
What you gonna do when the lake goes dry?
A   E
Sit on the bank and watch the crawdads die.
              B7   E
   Honey, sugar baby, mine.

Note Reading

There are no new notes in *Crawdad*.

I Was Born About Ten Thousand Years Ago

I was born a - bout ten thou-sand years a - go, There ain't

noth - ing in this world I do not know. I saw

Pet - er, Paul and Mos - es play - ing ring a - round the ros - es, And I'll

lick the guy that says it is - n't so.

```
         E                             B7
I saw Satan when he looked the Garden o'er,
                                    E
I saw Eve and Adam driven from the door.
         A
From behind the bushes peeping, saw the
         E
    apple they were eating,
         B7
And I'll swear that I'm the guy what ate
              E
    the core.
```

```
         E                             B7
I taught Samson how to use his mighty hands,

Showed Columbus how to reach this
                   E
    happy land.
         A                             E
And for Pharaoh's little kiddies, built all
    the pyramiddies,
         B7                    E
And then to Sahara carried all the sand.
```

```
         A                     B7
I taught Solomon his little ABCs,
                                    E
And was the first to eat Limburger cheese.

And while sailing down the bay with
              E
    Methuselah one day,
    B7                             E
I saved his flowing whiskers from the breeze.
```

```
         E                             B7
Queen Elizabeth, she fell in love with me.
                                    E
We were married in Milwaukee secretly.
         A
But I snuck around and shook her, to go
         E
    off with General Hooker,
    B7                             E
To fight mosquitos down in Tennessee.
```

Repeat first verse

Note Reading

There is one new note here.

D sharp

4/1

47

I Never Will Marry

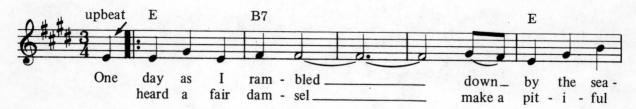

One day as I ram - bled _____ down by the sea -
heard a fair dam - sel _____ make a pit - i - ful

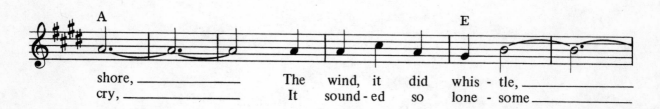

shore, _____ The wind, it did whis - tle, _____
cry, _____ It sound - ed so lone - some _____

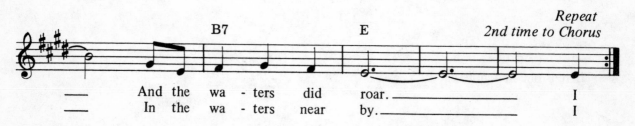

Repeat
2nd time to Chorus

And the wa - ters did roar. _____ I
In the wa - ters near by. _____ I

48

```
              E          B7
Chorus   I never will marry,
              E          A
         Nor be no man's wife.
                         E
         I intend to stay single
         B7         E
         The rest of my life


              E                B7
         My love's gone and left me,
              E      A
         He's the one I adore.
                         E
         He's gone where I never
         B7         E
         Will see him no more.
                              B7
         She plunged her dear body
              E      A
         In the water, so deep.
                              E
         She closed her pretty blue eyes
         B7         E
         In the water to sleep.   Chorus
```

Note Reading

There are no new notes here. Observe the tied notes extending over three measures. Make sure that you add up the total number of beats correctly.

The key signature of E major is four sharps:

F sharp, C sharp, G sharp and D sharp. We know all the notes needed to play the lower octave. For the middle octave we need one new note.

E Major Scale (Lower Octave)

E Major Scale (Middle Octave)

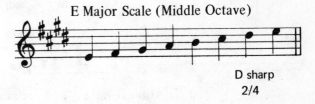

D sharp
2/4

49

The Key of C Major

The three main chords in the key of C major —the I, IV and V7 chords—are C, F and G7. F is played with one finger covering two strings.

You will have to lay your first finger as flat as possible while arching the other two to get this chord to sound clearly.

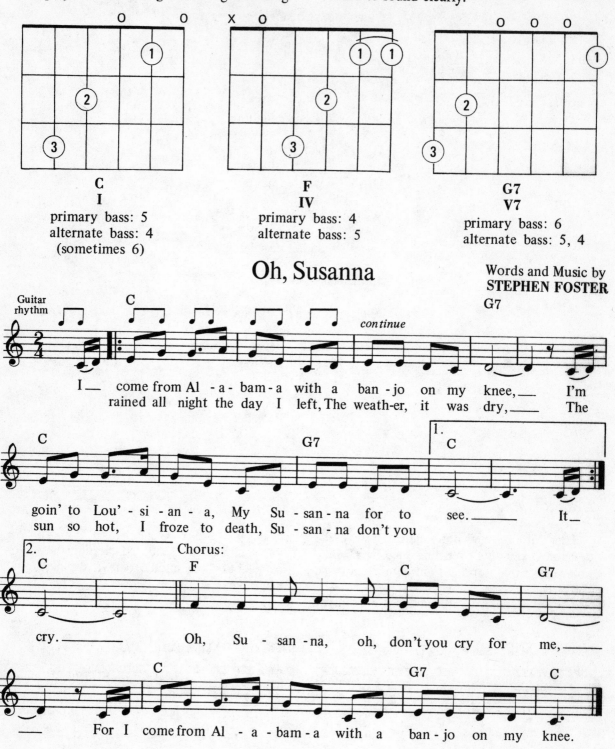

C
I
primary bass: 5
alternate bass: 4
(sometimes 6)

F
IV
primary bass: 4
alternate bass: 5

G7
V7
primary bass: 6
alternate bass: 5, 4

Oh, Susanna

Words and Music by
STEPHEN FOSTER

I come from Al - a - bam - a with a ban - jo on my knee,___ I'm
rained all night the day I left, The weath-er, it was dry,___ The

goin' to Lou' - si - an - a, My Su - san - na for to see.___ It
sun so hot, I froze to death, Su - san - na don't you

cry.___ Oh, Su - san - na, oh, don't you cry for me,___

— For I come from Al - a - bam - a with a ban - jo on my knee.

C
I had a dream the other night,
        G7
When everything was still.
C
I dreamed I saw Susanna
  G7   C
A-coming down the hill.

The buckwheat cake was in her hand,
        G7
The tear was in her eye.
    C
Says I, "I'm coming from the south,
 G7   C
Susanna, don't you cry."   *Chorus*

Note Reading

There is one new note in the key of C (F) and one that we have encountered only in the G major scale (C).

C
5/3

F
4/3

We see some new note values here as well: **sixteenth notes.** They may be written singly or in combinations of two or more.

Four sixteenth notes have the same total time value as two eighth notes or one quarter note.

Counting sixteenth notes for proper timing is a very rapid-fire affair under ordinary circumstances. One could say "one-uh-and-uh" to indicate the passing of four sixteenths, but it would be better to feel them as going twice as fast as eighth notes.

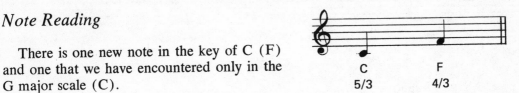

Count: 1 2 3 4   1 - and 2 - and 3 - and 4 - and   1 - uh-and-uh 2 - uh-and-uh 3 - uh- and-uh 4 - uh-and-uh

Another rhythmic figure appearing in *Oh, Susanna* for the first time is the **dotted-eighth– sixteenth** combination.

The dotted eighth is equivalent in time to three sixteenths. Again, counting three sixteenths and then playing the fourth sixteenth may be more confusing than helpful. It would be better to get the feel of the last sixteenth note as coming "just before" the next beat.

Continued→

Count: 1 - uh - and - uh   2 - uh - and - uh   3 - uh - and - uh   4 - uh - and - uh

Count: 1   2   3   4   1   *etc.*

Try playing *Oh, Susanna,* and see if you can put all of this together.

The Banks of the Ohio

I asked my love _____ to come with me, _____ To take a

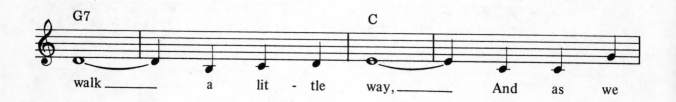

walk _____ a lit - tle way, _____ And as we

walked _____ we had a talk _____ A - bout our

52

1.　**To Chorus**　**2.Final Ending**

C　　　　　G7　　　C　　　　　　　　C

com - ing wed - ding day.＿＿＿ Then on - ly　　o.

　　　　　　　　　　C　　　　　G7　　C
Chorus　Then only say that you'll be mine,
　　　　　　　　　　　G7　　　　　C
　　　　　And in no other arms entwine,
　　　　　　　　　　　　　　　　　　　F
　　　　　Down beside where the waters flow,
　　　　　　　　　　　C　　　　G7 C
　　　　　Along the banks of the Ohio.

C　　　　　　　　G7　　　C
I asked your mother for you, dear,
　G7　　　　　　　　C
And she said you were too young.
　　　　　　　　　　F
Only say that you'll be mine—
　　　C　　　　G7　　　C
Happiness in my home you'll find.　*Chorus*

C　　　　　　　　　G7　　　C
I took her by her lily white hand,
　　　　　　　　　G7　　　　　　C
And led her down where the waters stand.
　　　　　　　　　　　　　F
I pitched her in without a sound,
　　　　　　　　　　C　　G7　　C
And watched her as she floated down.　*Chorus*

C　　　　　　　G7　　　C
I held a knife against her breast,
　G7　　　　　　　　C
As gently in my arms she pressed,
　　　　　　　　　　　　　　F
Crying, "Willie, oh Willie, don't murder me,
　　　C　　　G7 C
I'm unprepared for eternity."　*Chorus*

C　　　　　　　　　　　G7　　　C
I started back home 'twixt twelve and one,
　　　　　　　　　　G7　　　　　C
Crying, "My God, what have I done?
　　　　　　　　　　　　　　F
I've murdered my love—now woe betide—
　　　C　　　G7　　　C
Because she would not be my bride."　*Chorus*

Note Reading

No new notes or rhythmic problems.

The sixth note of the scale of C major is A. (We'll look at that scale after the next song.) The A minor chord is the **VI chord** of C. It is the relative minor of C.

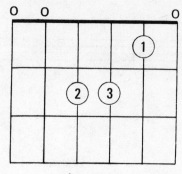

A minor

primary bass: 5
alternate bass: 6, 4

Relation to C: VI

Lincoln and Liberty

Campaign song for
Abraham Lincoln

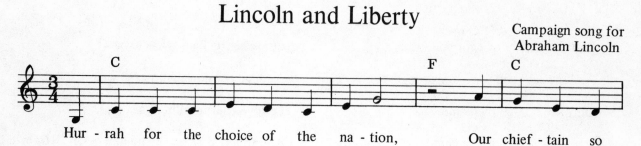

Hur - rah for the choice of the na - tion, Our chief - tain so

brave and so true,____ We'll go for the great re - for -

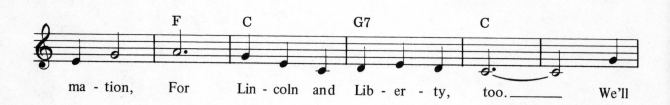

ma - tion, For Lin - coln and Lib - er - ty, too.____ We'll

go for the son of Ken - tuck - y,____ The he - ro of

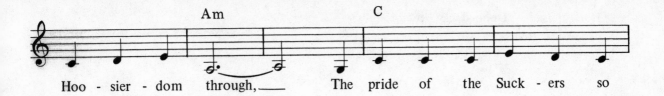

Hoo - sier - dom through,___ The pride of the Suck - ers so

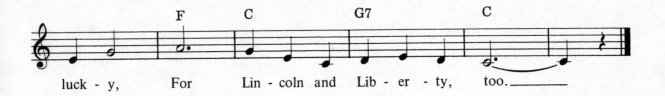

luck - y, For Lin - coln and Lib - er - ty, too.___

> C   F
> They'll find what by felling and mauling,
> C   Am
> Our rail-maker statesman can do;
> C
> For the people are everywhere calling
> F C   G7   C
> For Lincoln and Liberty, too.

> C   F
> Our David's good sling is unerring,
> C   Am
> The Slavocrat's giant he slew.
> C
> Then shout for the freedom preferring,
> F C   G7   C
> For Lincoln and Liberty, too.

> F
> Then up with the banner so glorious,
> C   Am
> The star-spangled red, white and blue.
> C
> We'll fight till our banner's victorious,
> F C   G7   C
> For Lincoln and Liberty, too.

> F
> We'll go for the son of Kentucky,
> C   Am
> The hero of Hoosierdom through,
> C
> The pride of the Suckers so lucky,
> F C   G7   C
> For Lincoln and Liberty, too.

Note Reading

Here are two notes we haven't come across in a while.

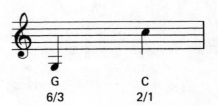

G
6/3

C
2/1

D minor is the **II chord** of C major. D7 is the **major II7** of C.

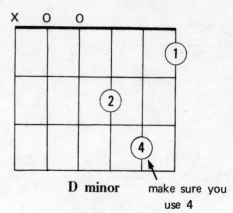

D minor make sure you use 4

primary bass: 4
alternate bass: 5

Deep Blue Sea

Deep   blue   sea,   ba - by,   deep   blue   sea,   Deep   blue

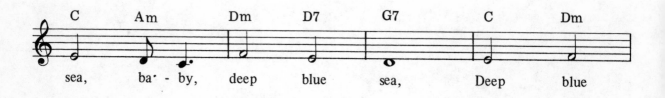

sea,   ba· - by,   deep   blue   sea,   Deep   blue

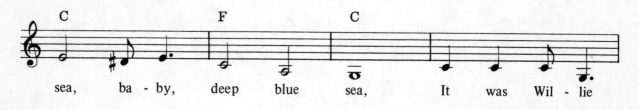

sea,   ba - by,   deep   blue   sea,   It   was   Wil - lie

what   got   drown-ded   in   the   deep   blue   sea.

C Dm C   F   C
Dig his grave with a silver spade,

   Dm C   Am Dm D7 G7
Dig his grave with a sil–ver spade,

C Dm C   F   C
Dig his grave with a silver spade,
                                   F
It was Willie what got drownded in the
     C   G7 C
       deep blue sea.

C Dm C   F   C
Lower him down with a golden chain,

   Dm   C   Am Dm D7 G7
Lower him down with a golden chain,

C Dm C   F   C
Lower him down with a golden chain,
                                   F
It was Willie what got drownded in the
     C   G7 C
       deep blue sea.

Repeat first verse

Note Reading

The key of C major has no sharps or flats in its key signature. If for melodic reasons a sharp is needed at some point, it must be written in directly in front of the affected note. This added sharp is called an **accidental.** It applies only to the notes in the measure where it is written. If it is needed in another measure, it must be written again.

Note the change in meter from $\frac{4}{4}$ (four beats per measure) to $\frac{2}{4}$ (two beats per measure) and back again to $\frac{4}{4}$ near the end of the song. This should not affect your playing of the accompaniment since you are playing a quarter-note strum. You just have to adjust your counting for that one shorter measure.

We know all the notes we need to play the C major scale.

C Major Scale

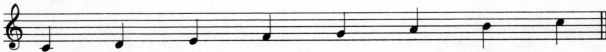

Transposing

We have now learned the I, IV and V7 chords (as well as a few others) in the five basic folk guitar keys: C, G, D, A and E. Any of these five keys can be the starting point for any song provided you know all the necessary chords. For three-chord songs (I, IV, V7) this is no problem. A song that is not comfortable to sing in the key of G with G, C and D7 chords, for example, would probably work very nicely in D with D, G and A7 chords. This process of changing a piece of music from one key to another is called **transposing.**

Here is how the I, IV and V7 chords line up against each other.

I	IV	V7
C	F	G7
G	C	D7
D	G	A7
A	D	E7
E	A	B7

For the II, III and VI chords (VII is rarely encountered) we will have to wait until other minor chords in addition to E minor, A minor and D minor have been learned.

2
BASS RUNS

Now that we have learned the basic chords and have some familiarity with note reading we can put these tools to use and begin to expand our technique. Chords and notes are building blocks, but it's what we do with them that counts.

Bass runs are single-note passages that serve to connect one chord to another. The bass runs take the place of the last two or three beats of one chord just before it changes to the next.

They vary the (so far) unchanging bass-chord or bass-chord-chord strum and also harmonize nicely with the melody as it is being sung.

The note reading done in the previous chapter will enable you to play all the runs without too much difficulty. If you do not remember some of the notes just look them up.

Remember to play all the melodies of the songs. Polish your reading skills.

Bass Runs in C— $\frac{4}{4}$ Time

Joe Turner

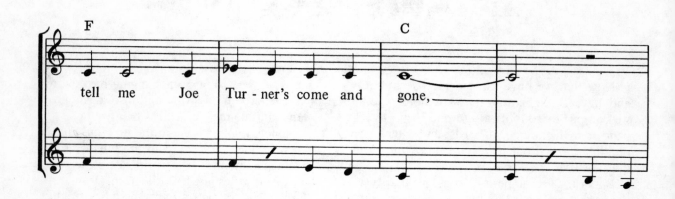

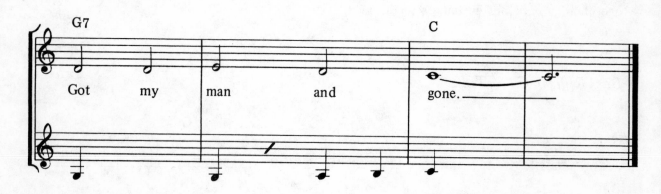

```
          C
He come with forty links of chain,
        F                        C
He come with forty links of chain,
 G7              C
Got my man and gone.


          C
They tell me Joe Turner's come and gone,
          F                          C
They tell me Joe Turner's come and gone,
 G7                 C
Left me to sing this song.


     C
Come like he never come before,
     F                        C
Come like he never come before,
 G7                 C
Got my man and gone.
```

To play the melody you need one new note.

E flat
4/1

Oleana

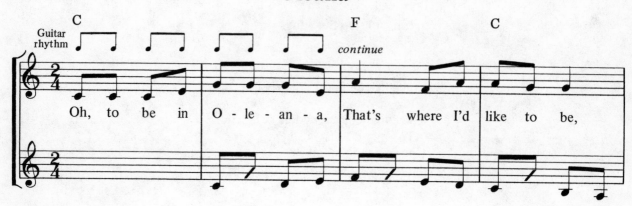

Oh, to be in O-le-an-a, That's where I'd like to be,

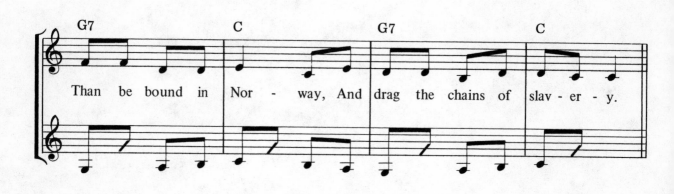

Than be bound in Nor-way, And drag the chains of slav-er-y.

Chorus:

O-le, O-le-an-a, O-le, O-le-an-a,

O - le, o - le, o - le, o - le, o - le, O - le - an - a.

        C
In Oleana land is free,
       F   C
The wheat and corn just plant themselves,
      G7   C
Then grow a good four feet a day,
      G7   C
While on your bed you rest yourself. *Chorus*

        C
Beer as sweet as Munchener
      F   C
Springs from the ground and flows away.
     G7   C
The cows all like to milk themselves,
     G7   C
And hens lay eggs ten times a day. *Chorus*

        C
Little roasted piggies just
      F   C
Rush about the city streets,
     G7   C
Inquiring so politely
     G7   C
If a slice of ham you'd like to eat. *Chorus*

        C
Say, if you'd begin to live,
      F   C
To Oleana you must go.
     G7   C
The poorest wretch in Norway
     G7   C
Becomes a duke in a year or so. *Chorus*

Remember to play a couple of measures before you start to sing. In that way the run in the first measure will be preceded by at least a full measure of the C chord.

On Top of Old Smoky

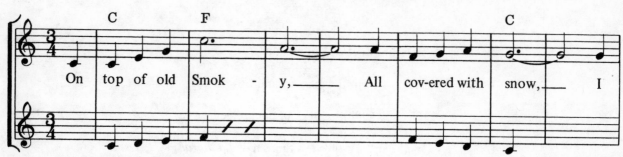

On top of old Smok - y,——— All cov-ered with snow,—— I

lost my true lov - er,——— By court - ing too slow.——

C   F
Well, courting is pleasure,
          C
And parting is grief,
          G7
But a false-hearted lover
          C
Is worse than a thief.

C   F
A thief, he will rob you,
          C
And take what you have.
          G7
But a false-hearted lover
          C
Will send you to your grave.

```
        C          F
And the grave will decay you,
        C
And turn you to dust.
          G7
And where is the young man
        C
A poor girl can trust?


        C          F
They'll hug you and kiss you,
        C
And tell you more lies
                        G7
Than the cross-ties on the railroad,
        C
Or the stars in the skies.


        C          F
They'll tell you they love you,
                C
Just to give your heart ease.
          G7
But the minute your back's turned,
                C
They'll court whom they please.


        C              F
So, come all you young maidens,
        C
And listen to me.
          G7
Never place your affection
        C
On a green willow tree.


        C          F
For the leaves, they will wither,
                C
And the roots, they will die.
                G7
And your true love will leave you,
                C
And you'll never know why.
```

It often happens that a chord is played for only one measure. When that occurs, as it does in measures 2, 10 and 22, to play the run in the normal three beat manner would eliminate using the chord. To avoid this situation we alter the rhythm of the chord and run combination to allow both to be heard. Check these measures carefully before beginning the song.

The Storms Are on the Ocean

heav-ens may cease to be.____ This world may lose its

Measure 22

mo - tion,__ love, If I prove__ false to__ thee.____

C	F	C
Now, who will shoe your pretty little feet?

G7   C
And who will glove your hand?

      F   C
Who will kiss your red rosy cheek,

   G7   C
Till I come back again. *Chorus*

      C   F   C
Poppa will shoe my pretty little feet,

G7   C
Momma will glove my hand.

          F   C
And you can kiss my red rosy cheek,

    G7   C
When you come back again. *Chorus*

       C   F   C
See that lonesome turtle dove

         G7   C
As he flies from pine to pine.

                F   C
He's mourning for his own true love,

         G7   C
Just the way I mourn for mine. *Chorus*

        C   F   C
I'll never go back on the ocean, love,

      G7   C
I'll never go back on the sea,

                  F   C
I'll never go back on the blue-eyed girl,

      G7   C
Till she goes back on me. *Chorus*

As you know, C is the only key that has no sharps or flats in its key signature. Starting with G, every key will have one or more sharp or flat in its signature. G has one sharp—F sharp. Watch out for the F sharps in the bass runs.

Mama Don't 'low

Ma - ma don't 'low no gui - tar pick - in' 'round here. _____

Ma - ma don't 'low no gui - tar pick - in' 'round here. _____

watch out

I don't care what Ma - ma don't 'low, Gon - na pick my gui - tar

68

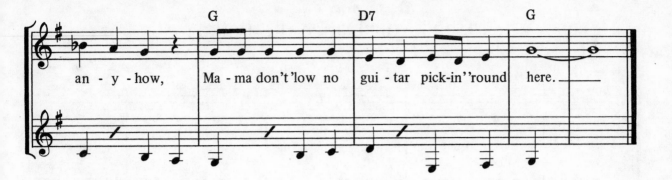

G
Mamma don't 'low no banjo playin' 'round
   here,
Mamma don't 'low no banjo playin' 'round
   D7
   here,
G
I don't care what mama don't 'low,
      C
Gonna play my banjo anyhow.
   G   D7
Mamma don't 'low no banjo playin' 'round
   G
   here.

G
Mama don't 'low no cigar smokin' 'round
   here,
Mama don't 'low no cigar smokin' 'round
   D7
   here.
G
I don't care what mama don't 'low,
      C
Gonna smoke my cigar anyhow.
   G   D7
Mama don't 'low no cigar smokin' 'round
   G
   here.

G
Mama don't 'low no midnight ramblin' 'round
   here,
Mama don't 'low no midnight ramblin' 'round
      D7
   here.
G
I don't care what mama don't 'low,
      C
Gonna ramble midnights anyhow.
   G   D7
Mama don't 'low no midnight ramblin' 'round
      G
   here.

G
Mama don't 'low no bass-run playin' 'round
   here,
Mama don't 'low no bass-run playin' 'round
      D7
   here.
G
I don't care what mama don't 'low,
      C
Gonna play them bass runs anyhow.
   G   D7
Mama don't 'low no bass-run playin' 'round
      G
   here.

There is a new note in the melody.
Watch out for the run from C to D7.

B flat
3/3

Can't You Dance the Polka?

```
       G            C
To Tiffany's I took her,
   D7            G
I did not mind expense.
                        C
I bought her two gold earrings,
       D7          G
They cost me fifty cents. *Chorus*


       G                    C
Says she, "You lime-juice sailor,
       D7                G
Now, see me home, you may."
                         C
But when we reached her cottage door,
       D7        G
She unto me did say: *Chorus*


       G                   C
"My young man he's a sailor,
        D7            G
With his hair cut short behind.
                      C
He wears a strip-ed jumper,
       D7               G
And sails the Black Ball Line." *Chorus*
```

Start playing a couple of measures before singing the first word since there is a run in measure one. Note that there are some phrases in this song where the chords change every measure. You now know what to do rhythmically to be able to play the chord and the run. However, it is not necessary to play every single run just because it is possible to do so. Remember, runs are supposed to add variety to your playing. If you play a run in every measure you may be defeating that purpose. The runs are all written out here for reference. Make your own choices.

Night-Herding Song

Oh, slow up do - gies, quit mov - ing a - round, You have

wan - dered and tram - pled all o - ver the ground. Oh, graze a - long

do - gies and feed kind of slow, And don't for - ev - er be

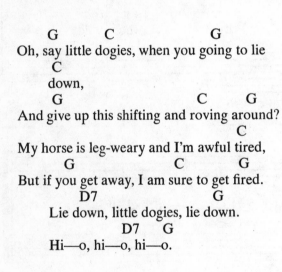

G   C   G
Oh, say little dogies, when you going to lie
 C
down,
 G   C G
And give up this shifting and roving around?
             C
My horse is leg-weary and I'm awful tired,
   G   C   G
But if you get away, I am sure to get fired.
   D7   G
  Lie down, little dogies, lie down.
     D7 G
  Hi—o, hi—o, hi—o.

     G   C   G
Lie still, little dogies, since you have lain
 C
down,
 G   C   G
And stretch away out on the big open ground.

Snore loud, little dogies, and drown the wild
      C
sound
 G   C   G
That will go away when the day rolls around.
     D7   G
  Lie still, little dogies, lie still.
      D7 G
  Hi—o, hi—o, hi—o.

The Bowery

Words by
CHARLES H. HOYT

Music by
PERCY GAUNT

Continued→

G   D7
I had walked but a block or two,
       G
When up came a fellow and me he knew.
    C♯ dim D7
Then a policeman came walking by,
      G
Chased him away, and I asked him why.
       D7
"Wasn't he pulling your leg?" said he.
     G
Said I, "He never laid hands on me!"
    C♯ dim D7
"Get off the Bowery, you fool!" said he.
     G
I'll never go there any more. *Chorus*

G   D7
Struck a place that they called a "dive,"
       G
I was in luck to get out alive.
     C♯ dim D7
When the policeman, he heard my woes,
       G
Saw my black eyes and my battered nose,
       D7
"You've been held up!" then the copper said.
        G
"No, sir! but I've been knocked down instead."
     C♯ dim D7
Then he just laughed, though I couldn't see why.
       G
I'll never go there any more. *Chorus*

Bass Runs in D—$\frac{4}{4}$ Time

 Remember the two sharps—F sharp and C sharp—in the key signature of D. They will show up in the runs.

Poor Howard

Poor How - ard's dead and gone, Left me here to

sing this song. | sing this song. | Poor How - ard's dead and gone.

Poor How - ard's dead and gone.

Left me here to sing this song.

D
Who's been here since I've been gone?
A7   **D**
Pretty little girl with a red dress on.

Who's been here since I've been gone?
A7   **D**
Pretty little girl with a red dress on.
   G   **D**
   Pretty little girl with a red dress on,
   A7   **D**
   Pretty little girl with a red dress on,
   G   **D**
   Pretty little girl with a red dress on,
   A7   **D**
   Left me here to sing this song.

D
Who's been here since I've been gone?
A7   **D**
Great big man with a derby on.

Who's been here since I've been gone?
A7   **D**
Great big man with a derby on.
   G   **D**
   Great big man with a derby on,
   A7   **D**
   Great big man with a derby on,
   G   **D**
   Great big man with a derby on,
   A7   **D**
   Left me here to sing this song.

77

Streets of Glory

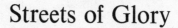

I'm gon-na walk the streets of Glo - ry, I'm gon-na

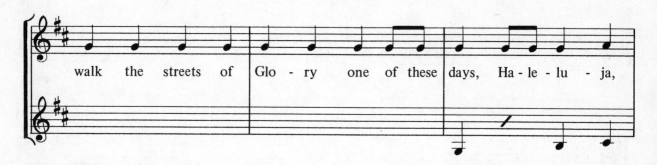

walk the streets of Glo - ry one of these days, Ha - le - lu - ja,

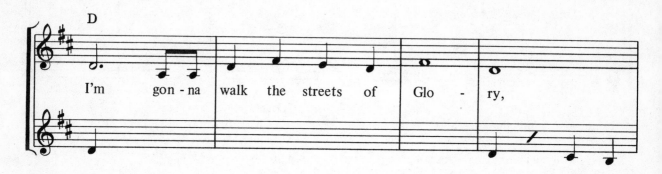

I'm gon - na walk the streets of Glo - ry,

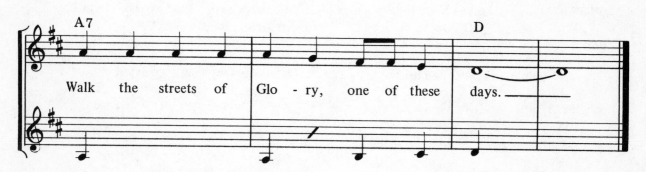

Walk the streets of Glo - ry, one of these days. ___

78

D
I'm gonna tell God how you treat me,
G
I'm gonna tell God how you treat me

One of these days, hallelujah!
D
I'm gonna tell God how you treat me,
A7   D
Tell God how you treat me one of these days.

D
I'm gonna walk and talk with Jesus,
G
I'm gonna walk and talk with Jesus

One of these days, hallelujah!
D
I'm gonna walk and talk with Jesus,
A7   D
Walk and talk with Jesus one of these days.

D
I'm gonna sit at the welcome table,
G
I'm gonna sit at the welcome table

One of these days, hallelujah!
D
I'm gonna sit at the welcome table,
A7   D
Sit at the welcome table one of these days.

Repeat first verse

Green Grow the Lilacs

Green grow the li - lacs, all spark - ling with dew, I'm

lone - ly my dar - ling since part - ing with you. But

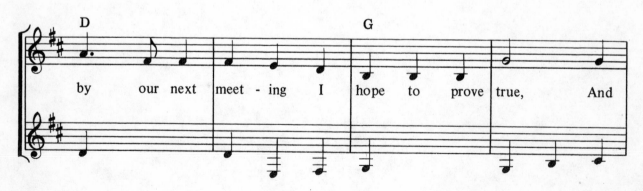

by our next meet - ing I hope to prove true, And

change the green li - lacs to the red, white and blue.

D
I used to have a sweetheart, but now I have none.
                                    A7
Since she's gone and left me, I care not for one.
D   G
Since she's gone and left me, contented I'll be,
D   A7   D
For she loves another one better than me.

D
I passed my love's window, both early and late.
                             A7
The look that she gave me, it made my heart ache.
          D   G
Oh, the look that she gave me was painful to see,
          D   A7   D
For she loves another one better than me.

          D
I wrote my love letters in rosy red lines.
                           A7
She sent me an answer all twisted in twines,
          D   G
Saying, "Keep your love letters and don't waste your time,
          D   A7   D
Just you write to your love and I'll write to mine."

Repeat first verse

81

Pay strict attention to the guitar rhythm in *The Jug of Punch*. It is a variation of the $\frac{3}{4}$ strum consisting of three bass-chord strums per measure—six eighth notes in all. It gives a livelier feeling to this song. The runs all fall on the last two (5th and 6th) eighth notes of their respective measures.

The Jug of Punch

As I was sit - ting with a jug and spoon, On one fine morn in the month of June. A bird - ie sang on an i - vy bunch, And the song he sang was "The Jug of Punch." Too ra loo ra loo, Too ra loo ra loo, Too ra loo ra loo, Too ra loo ra loo. A

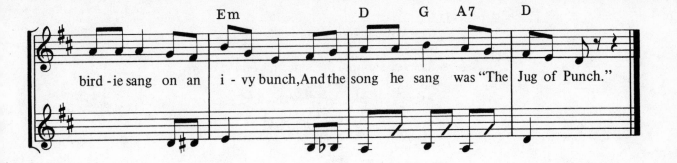

bird -ie sang on an | i - vy bunch, And the | song he sang was "The | Jug of Punch."

     D
What more diversion can a man desire,
         A7   D
Than to court a girl by a neat turf fire?
               Em
A Kerry pippin and the crack and crunch,
    D   G A7 D
And on the table a jug of punch.

        A7   D
Chorus   Too ra loo ra loo, too ra loo ra loo,
           A7   D
Too ra loo ra loo, too ra loo ra loo.
                 Em
A Kerry pippin and the crack and crunch,
     D   G A7 D
And on the table a jug of punch.

      D
All ye noble lords drink your nectar wine,
       A7   D
And the quality drink their claret fine.
                 Em
I'll give them all the grapes in the bunch,
    D   G A7   D
For a jolly pull at the jug of punch.

        A7   D
Chorus   Too ra loo ra loo, too ra loo ra loo,
           A7   D
Too ra loo ra loo, too ra loo ra loo.
                 Em
I'll give them all the grapes in the bunch,
     D   G A7   D
For a jolly pull at the jug of punch.

Continued→

D
The learned doctors with all their art,
    A7   D
Sadness cannot cure, once it's on the heart.
        Em
Even a cripple forgets his hunch,
     D   G A7 D
When he's safe outside of a jug of punch.

     A7 D
Chorus Too ra loo ra loo, too ra loo ra loo,
       A7   D
Too ra loo ra loo, too ra loo ra loo.
        Em
Even a cripple forgets his hunch,
     D G A7 D
When he's safe outside of a jug of punch.

D
If I drink too much, well my money's my own,
  A7   D
And them's don't like me can leave me alone.
         Em
But I'll tune my fiddle and I'll rosin my bow,
   D G A7   D
And I'll be welcome wherever I go.

     A7 D
Chorus Too ra loo ra loo, too ra loo ra loo,
       A7   D
Too ra loo ra loo, too ra loo ra loo,
          Em
But I'll tune my fiddle and I'll rosin my bow,
     D G A7   D
And I'll be welcome wherever I go.

D
Ah, but when I'm dead and in my grave,
    A7   D
No costly tombstone will I crave.
                            Em
Just lay me down in my native peat,
       D   G   A7   D
With a jug of punch at my head and feet.

            A7   D
Chorus   Too ra loo ra loo, too ra loo ra loo,
               A7   D
Too ra loo ra loo, too ra loo ra loo.
                          Em
Just lay me down in my native peat,
       D   G   A7   D
With a jug of punch at my head and **feet**.

Bass Runs in A—$\frac{4}{4}$ Time

Remember the three sharps—F sharp, C sharp and G sharp—in the key signature of A.

They will show up in the runs.

Play E7 this way. It gives a fuller sound.

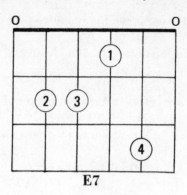

E7

primary bass: 6
alternate bass: 5, 4

All Night Long

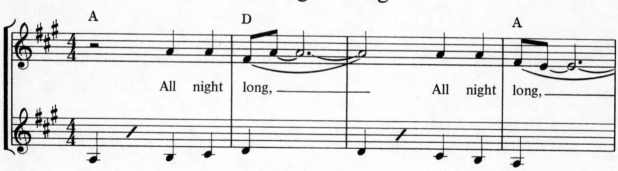

All night long, _____ All night long, _____

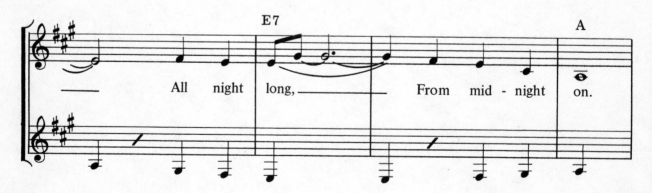

_____ All night long, _____ From mid - night on.

Down by the sta-tion,_____ read-y to go,_____

_____ If the train don't come,_____ some-thing's wrong down the road.

A D A
If I live and don't get killed,
    E7   A
I'll make my home in Louisville.
    D   A
In Louisville, in Louisville,
    E7   A
If I live and don't get killed.

A   D   A
I'd rather be dead and in my grave,
        E7   A
Than in this town, treated this way.
    D   A
Treated this way, treated this way,
        E7   A
Than in this town, treated this way.

A   D   A
If anyone asks you who wrote this song,
        E7   A
Tell 'em I did—I sing it all night long.
    D   A
All night long, all night long,
        E7   A
Tell 'em I did—I sing it all night long.

Boatman Dance

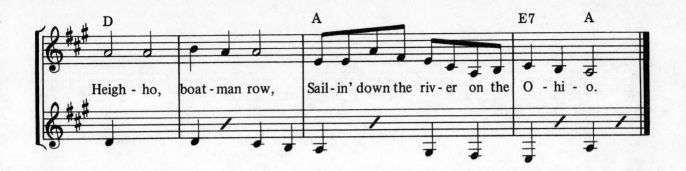

Heigh - ho, boat-man row, Sail-in' down the riv - er on the O - hi - o.

A
When the boatman gets on shore,
      E7 A
He spends his money and he works for more.
  Chorus

A
Never saw a pretty girl in my life,
    E7
But that she was a boatman's wife.

  Chorus

 A
When the boatman blows his horn,
      E7 A
Look out, old man, your daughter is gone.
  Chorus

 A
Sky-blue jacket and a tarpaulin hat,
      E7 A
Look out, boys, for the nine-tail cat.

  Chorus

Who's Gonna Shoe Your Pretty Little Foot?

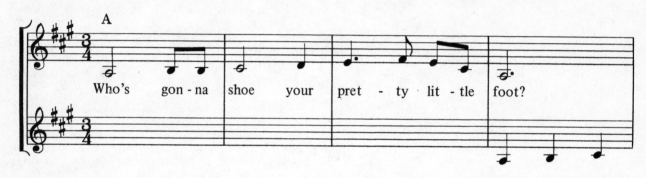

Who's gon-na shoe your pret-ty lit-tle foot?

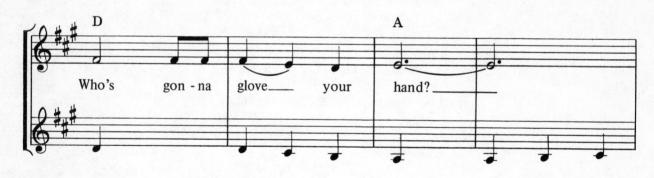

Who's gon-na glove___ your hand?___

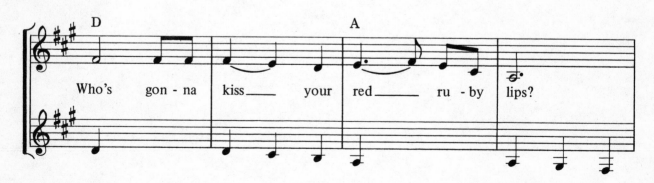

Who's gon-na kiss___ your red___ ru-by lips?

Who's gon - na be your man? _____

A
Papa's gonna shoe my pretty little foot,
　D　　　　　　　　A
Mama's gonna glove my hand.
　D　　　　　　　　A
Sister's gonna kiss my red ruby lips,
E7　　　　　　A
I don't need no man.

A
I don't need no man,
　D　　　　　　A
I don't need no man.
　　D　　　　　　　　A
Sister's gonna kiss my red ruby lips,
E7　　　　　A
I don't need no man.

　　　　A
The longest train I ever did see
　　　　D　　　　A
Was a hundred coaches long.
　　　　D　　　　　A
The only woman I ever did love
　　　E7　　　　　A
Was on that train and gone.

　A
On that train and gone,
　D　　　　　　　A
On that train and gone.
　　D　　　　　A
The only woman I ever did love
　　　E7　　　　　　A
Was on that train and gone.

Abdullah starts with a bass run leading into the singing.

Abdullah Bulbul Amir

The ranks of the Pro - phet are hard - y and bold, And quite un - ac - cus - tomed to fear. ___ But the brav - est of all was a man, I am told, Named Ab - dul - lah Bul - bul A - mir. ___

A   E7   A
When they needed a man to encourage the van,
      D   A
Or to harass the foe from the rear,
      E7   A
Storm fort or redoubt, they had only to shout
      E7   A
For Abdullah Bulbul Amir.

A   E7   A
Now, the heroes were plenty and well known
    to fame,
      D   A
Who fought in the ranks of the Czar.
      E7   A
But the bravest of these was a man by the name
      E7   A
Of Ivan Skavinsky Skivar.

A   E7   A
He could imitate Pushkin, play poker and pool,
      D   A
And strum on the Spanish guitar.
      E7   A
In fact, quite the cream of the Muscovite team
      E7   A
Was Ivan Skavinsky Skivar.

A   E7   A
One day this bold Russian had shouldered
    his gun,
      D   A
And donned his most truculent sneer.
      E7   A
Downtown he did go, where he trod on the toe
      E7   A
Of Abdullah Bulbul Amir.

A   E7   A
"Young man," quoth Bulbul, "has your life
    grown so dull,
          D   A
That you're anxious to end your career?
      E7   A
Vile infidel, know, you have trod on the toe
      E7   A
Of Abdullah Bulbul Amir."

A   E7   A
Said Ivan, "My friend, your remarks in the end,
      D   A
Will avail you but little, I fear.
      E7   A
For you ne'er will survive to repeat them alive,
      E7   A
Mister Abdullah Bulbul Amir."

A   E7   A
They fought all that night 'neath the yellow
    moonlight,
      D   A
The din, it was heard from afar.
      E7   A
And huge multitudes came, so great was
    the fame
      E7   A
Of Abdul and Ivan Skivar.

A   E7   A
As Abdul's long knife was extracting the life,
      D   A
In fact he had shouted, "Huzzah!"
      E7   A
He felt himself struck by that wily Kalmuck,
      E7   A
Count Ivan Skavinsky Skivar.

A   E7   A
There's a tomb made of gold where the Blue
    Danube rolls,
      D   A
And 'graved there in characters clear,
      E7   A
Is, "Stranger, when passing, oh, pray for
    the soul
      E7   A
Of Abdullah Bulbul Amir."

A   E7   A
A Muscovite maiden, her lone vigil keeps,
      D   A
'Neath the light of the pale polar star.
      E7   A
And the name that she murmurs so oft
    as she weeps,
      E7   A
Is Ivan Skavinsky Skivar.

Remember the four sharps—F sharp, C sharp, G sharp, and D sharp—in the key signature of E. They will show up in the runs.

This Train

94

  E
This train don't carry no gamblers—this train.
                                          B7
This train don't carry no gamblers—this train.
  E
This train don't carry no gamblers,
  A   E
No hypocrites, no midnight ramblers.
           B7   E
This train is bound for Glory—this train.

  E
This train is built for speed now—this train.
                                   B7
This train is built for speed now—this train.
  E
This train is built for speed now,
  A   E
Fastest train you ever did see now.
           B7   E
This train is bound for Glory—this train.

  E
This train don't carry no liars—this train.
                             B7
This train don't carry no liars—this train.
  E
This train don't carry no liars,
  A   E
No con men and no high flyers.
           B7   E
This train is bound for Glory—this train.

  E
This train's free transportation—this train.
                                B7
This train's free transportation—this train.
  E
This train's free transportation,
  A   E
You won't find discrimination.
           B7   E
This train is bound for Glory—this train.

No Hiding Place

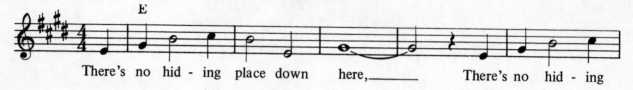

There's no hid - ing place down here,_____ There's no hid - ing

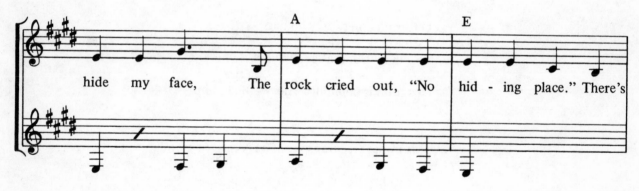

place down here._____ Oh, I ran to the rock to

watch out!

hide my face, The rock cried out, "No hid - ing place." There's

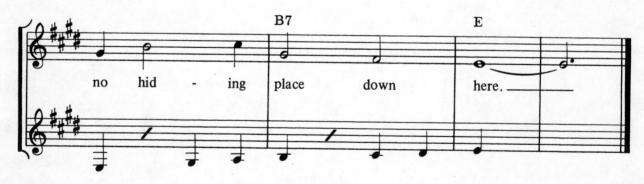

no hid - ing place down here._____

      E
The rock cried, "I'm burning, too."
                        B7
The rock cried, "I'm burning, too."
      E
The rock cried out, "I'm burning, too."
 A   E
I want to go to heaven the same as you."
            B7   E
There's no hiding place down here.

      E
Sinner man, he stumbled and fell.
                      B7
Sinner man, he stumbled and fell.
        E
Oh, the sinner man stumbled and he fell.
 A   E
Tried to get to heaven but he had to go to hell.
            B7   E
There's no hiding place down here.

Hard Is the Fortune of All Womankind

Hard is the for - tune of__ all wom - an - kind,__ They're

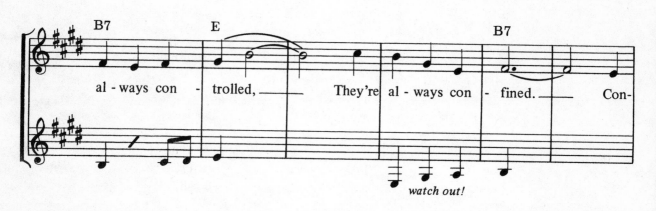

al - ways con - trolled,__ They're al - ways con - fined.__ Con-

watch out!

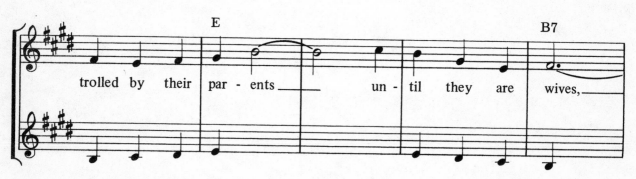

trolled by their par - ents __ un - til they are wives,__

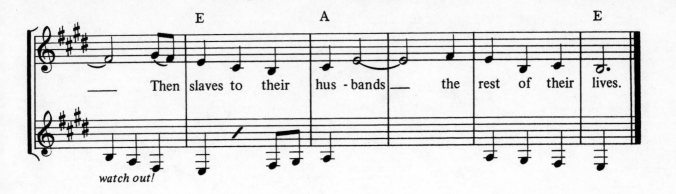

watch out!

E
"Oh, I am a poor girl, my fortune is sad.
B7   E   B7
I have always been courted by the wagoner's lad.
          E   B7
He courted me daily, by night and by day,
      E   A   E
And now he is loaded and going away.

          E
"Your horses are hungry, go feed them some hay.
      B7   E   B7
Come sit down beside me as long as you stay."
          E   B7
"My horses ain't hungry, they won't eat your hay,
      E   A   E
So, fare you well, darling, I'll be on my way."

          E
"Your wagon needs greasing, your whip is to mend.
      B7   E   B7
Come sit down here by me as long as you can."
          E   B7
"My wagon is greasy, my whip's in my hand.
      E   A   E
So, fare you well, darling, no longer to stand."

You may need your capo on the third or fourth fret for *Billy Barlow*.

Billy Barlow

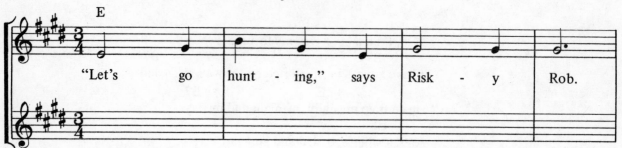

"Let's go hunt - ing," says Risk - y Rob.

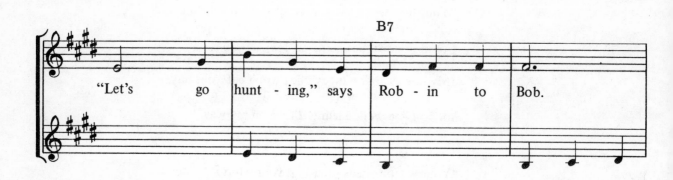

"Let's go hunt - ing," says Rob - in to Bob.

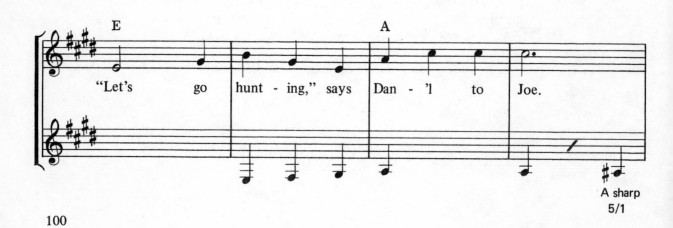

"Let's go hunt - ing," says Dan - 'l to Joe.

A sharp
5/1

100

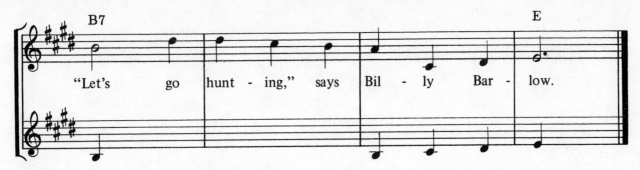

"Let's go hunt - ing," says Bil - ly Bar - low.

E
"What shall I hunt?" says Risky Rob.
              B7
"What shall I hunt?" says Robin to Bob.
E   A
"What shall I hunt?" says Dan'l to Joe.
B7   E
"Hunt for a rat," says Billy Barlow.

E
"How shall I get him?" says Risky Rob.
              B7
"How shall I get him?" says Robin to Bob.
E   A
"How shall I get him?" says Dan'l to Joe.
B7   E
"Borrow a gun," says Billy Barlow.

A
"How shall I haul him?" says Risky Rob.
              B7
"How shall I haul him?" says Robin to Bob.
E   A
"How shall I haul him?" says Dan'l to Joe.
B7   E
"Borrow a wagon," says Billy Barlow.

E
"How shall we divide him?" says Risky Rob.
              B7
"How shall we divide him?" says Robin to Bob.
E   A
"How shall we divide him?" says Dan'l to Joe.
B7   E
"Watch how I do it," says Billy Barlow.

E
"I'll take shoulder," says Risky Rob.
              B7
"I'll take take side," says Robin to Bob.
E   A
"I'll take ham," says Dan'l to Joe.
B7   E
"Tail bone mine," says Billy Barlow.

E
"How shall we cook him?" says Risky Rob.
              B7
"How shall we cook him?" says Robin to Bob.
E   A
"How shall we cook him?" says Dan'l to Joe.
B7   E
"Each as you like it," says Billy Barlow.

E
"I'll broil shoulder," says Risky Rob.
              B7
"I'll fry side," says Robin to Bob.
E   A
"I'll boil ham," says Dan'l to Joe.
B7   E
"Tail bone raw," says Billy Barlow.

3
ARPEGGIOS

Just as the fingers of the right hand may play individual notes of the melody, so may they play individual notes of the chord. When the notes of a chord are played one at a time (or in various combinations) instead of being plucked simultaneously, the resulting pattern is known as an **arpeggio.**

There are as many arpeggio patterns as there are sequences of strings which may be played by the right hand. We will explore some of the basic arpeggios in this chapter.

Arpeggios in $\frac{4}{4}$ and $\frac{2}{4}$ Time

- Finger a D chord.
- Play the basic four beat, thumb-finger strum.

alternate basses

- Now subdivide the last two quarter notes of each measure into four eighth notes, using the thumb and fingers one, two and three as shown. Make sure that the timing is accurate. The "three-and four-and" of the arpeggio takes the same time to play as the "one two" of the first part of the measure.

Right hand T   F   T   1   2   3   T   F   T   1   2   3
Count: 1   2   3 - and 4 - and   1   2   3 - and 4 - and

My Home's Across the Smoky Mountains

My home's a -
cross the Smok - y Moun - tains, My
home's a - cross the Smok - y Moun -
tains, My home's a - cross the Smok - y
Moun - tains, And I'll nev - er get to
see you an - y - more, more, more, And I'll

nev - er get to see you an - y - more. _____

D
Goodbye, honey, sugar darling.
  A7   D
Goodbye, honey, sugar darling.

Goodbye, honey, sugar darling,
    Em   A7   D
And I'll never get to see you anymore, more,
    more;
  Em   A7   D
I'll never get to see you anymore.

D
I'm bound to cross that lonesome valley.
  A7   D
I'm bound to cross that lonesome valley.

I'm bound to cross that lonesome valley,
      Em   A7   D
And I'll never get to see you anymore, more,
      more;
  Em   A7   Đ
I'll never get to see you anymore.

          D
So, don't you grieve for me, my darling.
  A7   D
Don't you grieve for me, my darling.

Don't you grieve for me, my darling,
      Em   A7   D
And I'll never get to see you anymore, more, more;
    Em   A7   D
I'll never get to see you anymore.

- • Finger an A chord.

- • Play the basic four-beat, thumb-finger strum. This time, however, the four beats are written as eighth notes so that there are four bass-chord strums per measure.

Count: 1 - and 2 - and 3 - and 4 - and 1 - and 2 - and 3 - and 4 - and

This does not affect anything except your counting.

Now subdivide the second and fourth beats (that is, eighth notes numbers 3,4,7,8) into sixteenth notes in exactly the same manner as with the previous arpeggio. Your right hand makes the same moves—it's just a question of counting.

| Right hand | T | F | T | 1 | 2 | 3 | T | F | T | 1 | 2 | 3 | T | F | T | 1 | 2 | 3 | T | F | T | 1 | 2 | 3 |
| Count: | 1 | and | 2 | - | and | - | 3 | and | 4 | - | and | - | 1 | and | 2 | - | and | - | 3 | and | 4 | - | and | - |

Songs for which the feel of the accompaniment would have been an eighth-note, bass-chord strum take this rhythmic pattern.

The Desperado

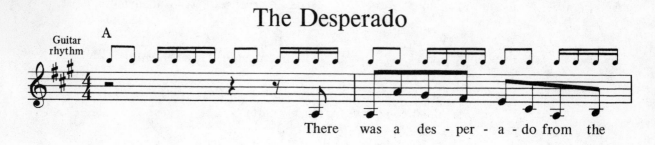

There was a des - per - a - do from the

wild and wool - ly west.   He came in from Chi - ca - go just to

give the west a rest.   He wore a big som - bre -ro and two

guns be-neath his vest,   And ev -'ry-where he went he gave his

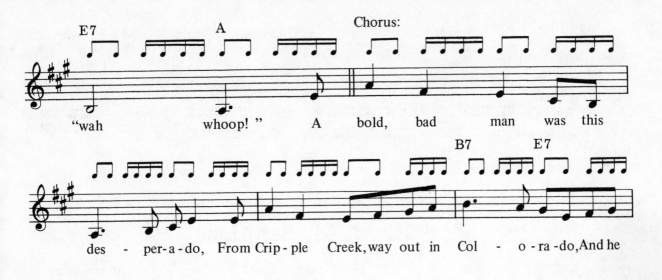

"wah whoop! " A bold, bad man was this

des - per-a-do, From Crip-ple Creek, way out in Col - o -ra-do, And he

walked a - round like a big tor - na - do, And

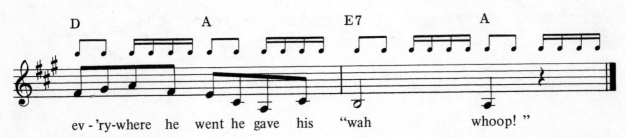

ev - 'ry-where he went he gave his "wah whoop! "

A
He came to Coney Island just to take in all

the sights,
B7
He went up to the loop-the-loop that scaled
E7
the tallest heights.
A
It got him so excited that he shot out all

the lights,
D   A   E7
And everywhere he went he gave his "wah
A
whoop!" *Chorus*

A
A great big fat policeman came a-walking

down his beat.
B7
He saw the desperado come on trucking down
E7
the street.
A
He took him by the collar and he took him

by the seat,
D   A   E7
And put him where he couldn't give his "wah
A
whoop!" *Chorus*

Arpeggios for songs in $\frac{2}{4}$ time are generally the same as for those in $\frac{4}{4}$. Usually they are of the eighth and sixteenth note variety.

In *Saro Jane,* however, a new element is introduced: a chord change on the second beat of some measures. The first beat is the bass chord and the second beat is the arpeggio.

Rock About, My Saro Jane

I've got a wife and a-

five lit-tle chil-lun, Be-lieve I'll make a trip on the Big— Mac-mil-lan.

Chorus:

Oh, Sa - ro Jane. Oh, there's noth-ing to

do but to sit down and sing, And rock a-bout, my

Sa - ro Jane. Oh, rock a-bout my

Sa - ro Jane, Oh, rock a-bout my Sa - ro

Jane. Oh, there's noth-ing to do but to sit down and

sing, And rock a-bout my Sa - ro Jane._____

Am   C
Boiler busted and the whistle done blowed,
                          Am
The head captain done fell overboard. *Chorus*

Am   C
Engine gave a crack and the whistle gave a squall,
                          Am
The engineer gone through the hole in the wall. *Chorus*

Am   C
Yankees built boats for to shoot them rebels,
                          Am
My musket's loaded and I'm gonna hold her level. *Chorus*

Slower moving ballads sound well when an
all-arpeggio pattern is used.

T 1 2 3 T 1 2 3

alternate basses throughout

The Water Is Wide

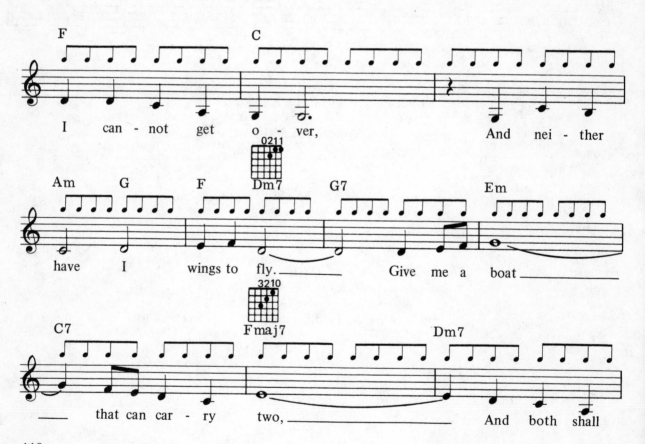

The wa-ter is wide,

I can - not get o - ver, And nei - ther

have I wings to fly. Give me a boat

that can car - ry two, And both shall

110

row, _____ My love and I. _____

*"sus 4" means "suspended 4" - here the note C is "suspended" from the Dm7 into the G7, where as the 4th of G it eliminates the 3rd, B.

  C   F   C
A ship there is and she sails the sea,
    Am G F Dm7 G7
She's loaded deep as deep can be.
    Em C7   F maj 7 Dm7
But not so deep as the love I'm in,
    G7sus4 G7   C
And I know not how   to sink or swim.

  C   F   C
I leaned my back against a young oak,
    Am G F Dm7 G7
Thinking he was a trusty tree.
    Em C7   F maj 7 Dm7
But first he bended and then he broke,
    G7sus4 G7   C
And thus did my   false love to me.

  C   F   C
I put my hand into some soft bush,
    Am G F   DM7 G7
Thinking the sweetest flower to find.
    Em C7   F maj 7 Dm7
The thorn, it stuck me to the bone,
    G7sus4 G7   C
And, oh, I left   that flower alone.

  C   F   C
Oh, love is handsome and love is fine,
    Am G F Dm7 G7
Gay as a jewel when first it's new.
    Em C7   F maj 7 Dm7
But love grows old and waxes cold,
    G7sus4 G7   C
And fades away   like summer dew.

Here is another all-eighth-note pattern.

T 1 2 1 3 1 2 1   T 1 2 1 3 1 2 1   T 1 2 1 3 1 2 1   T 1 2 1 3 1 2 1

alternate basses

John Riley

Fair young maid   all   in   the

gar - den, _____ Strange young man   pass   her   by. _____

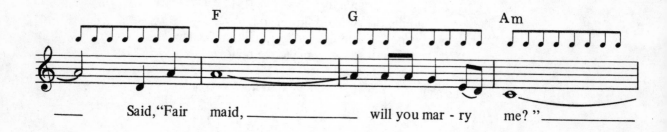

__   Said, "Fair   maid, _____ will you mar - ry   me? "

__   This then,   sir, _____ was her re - ply. _____

```
        Dm           G      Dm
"Oh no, kind sir, I cannot marry,
                      G      Dm
For I've a love who sails the sea.
            F G            Am
He's been gone for these seven years.
         Em Dm          G Dm
Still no man    shall marry me."


Dm              G    Dm
"What if he's in battle slain?
                      G        Dm
Or drowned in the deep salt sea?
            F G           Am
What if he's found another love,
              Em Dm            G Dm
And that they    both married be?"


Dm              G    Dm
"If he's in some battle slain,
                      G        Dm
I'll die when the moon doth wane.
            F  G              Am
If he's drowned in the deep salt sea,
            Em Dm           G Dm
I'll be true    to his memory.


Dm              G    Dm
"If he's found another love,
                      G      Dm
And if they both married be,
            F G            Am
Then I wish them happiness,
              Em Dm             G Dm
Where they dwell    across the sea."


          Dm        G      Dm
He picked her up all in his arms,
                      G        Dm
Kisses gave her, one, two, three.
            F G               Am
"Weep no more, my own true love,
              Em Dm          G Dm
"I'm your long    lost John Riley."
```

Now add a thumb beat on the fourth beat.
The thumb may either play another note of the
chord or a new note leading to the next chord.

The Cruel War

114

morn - ing till night.

1.
I'll

Final Ending
yes.

              G   Em   D7sus4   G
I'll go to your captain, get down upon my knees

          Em   C   D7sus4   G
Ten thousand gold guineas I'll give for your release.

          G   Em   D7sus4   G
Ten thousand gold guineas, it grieves my heart so.

            Em   C   D7sus4   G
Won't you let me go with you?—Oh no, my love, no.

          G   Em   D7sus4   G
Your captain calls for you, it grieves my heart so.

            Em   C   D7sus4   G
Won't you let me go with you?—Oh no, my love, no.

           G   Em   D7sus4   G
Your waist is too slender, your fingers are too small,

              Em   C   D7sus4   G
Your cheeks are too rosy to face the cannonball.

          G   Em   D7sus4   G
Oh, Johnny, my Johnny, I think you are unkind,

     Em   C   D7sus4   G
I love you far better than all other mankind.

          G   Em   D7sus4   G
I'll pull back my hair, men's clothes I'll put on,

     Em   C   D7sus4   G
I'll pass for your comrade as we march along.

          G   Em   D7sus4   G
I'll pass for your comrade and none will ever guess.

            Em   C   D7sus4   G
Won't you let me go with you?—Oh yes, my love, yes.

An all-arpeggio pattern of sixteenth notes.

Play the chords as indicated but follow the first note of each group of sixteenths. It may not always be the "customary" bass note.

Down by the Sally Gardens

Words by
WILLIAM BUTLER YEATS

Music
TRADITIONAL

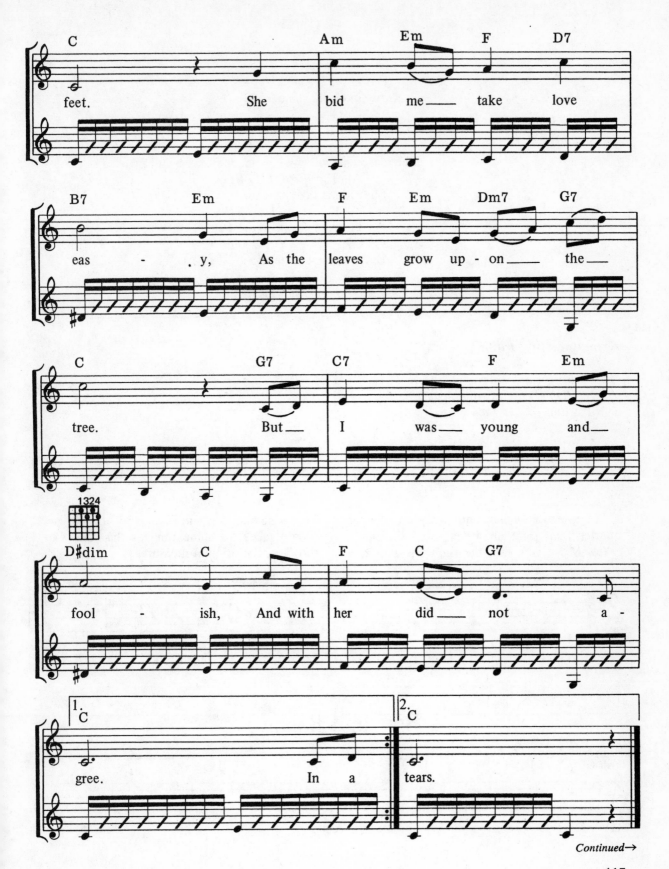

Continued→

```
        C  G      F C
In a field by the river,
       F  C  G7    C
My love and I did stand.
              G    F     C
And on my leaning shoulder
       F    C  G7       C
She placed her snow-white hand.
    Am Em F    D7 B7 Em
She bid me take life easy,
         F   Em  Dm7 G7 C
As the grass grows on the weirs.
G7 C7    F     Em D♯dim  C
But I was young and fool  —  ish,
        F  C G7     C
And now am full of tears.
```

Arpeggios in ¾ Time

- Finger a C chord.
- Play the basic three-beat, bass-chord-chord strum.

We now subdivide an entire measure of three quarter notes into an arpeggio of six eighth notes. Make sure that the timing is accurate.

The "one-and two-and three-and" of the arpeggio takes the same time as the "one two three" of the original measure.

T F F   T 1 2 3 2 1   T F F   T 1 2 3 2 1   T F F   T 1 2 3 2 1

Bow and Balance

There

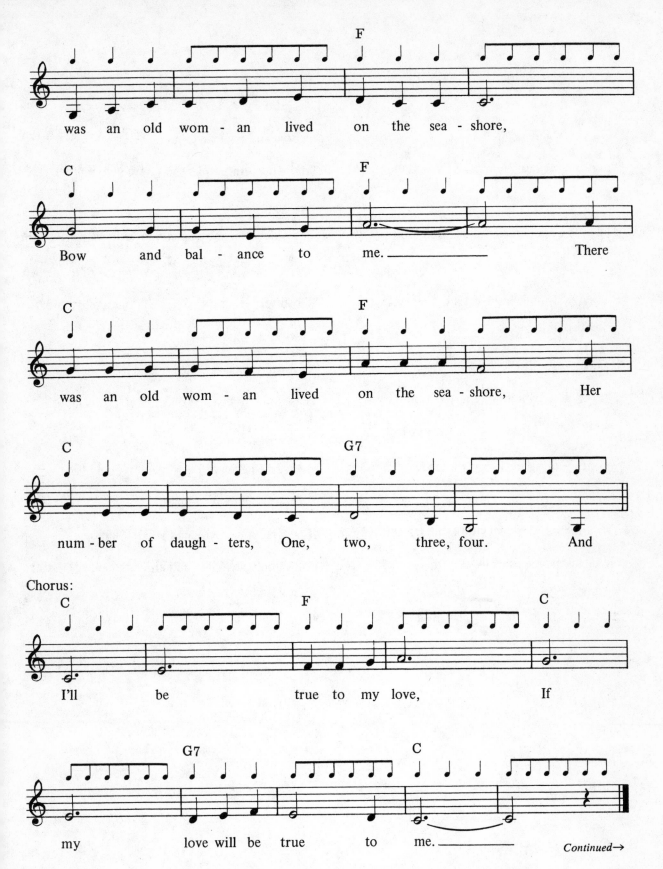

was an old wom-an lived on the sea-shore,

C ... **F**

Bow and bal-ance to me. _____ There

C ... **F**

was an old wom-an lived on the sea-shore, Her

C ... **G7**

num-ber of daugh-ters, One, two, three, four. And

Chorus:

C ... **F** ... **C**

I'll be true to my love, If

G7 ... **C**

my love will be true to me. _____ *Continued→*

```
        C                              F
There was a young man who came there to

   see them,
        C                    F
Bow and balance to me.
        C                              F
There was a young man who came there to

   see them,
        C                    G7
The oldest daughter got stuck on him. Chorus
```

```
        C                        F
He bought for the youngest a beaver hat,
        C                F
   Bow and balance to me.
        C                        F
He bought for the youngest a beaver hat,
        C                G7
The oldest daughter got angry at that. Chorus
```

```
        C                          F
"Oh sister, oh sister, let's walk the sea shore."
        C                 F
   Bow and balance to me.
        C                          F
"Oh sister, oh sister, let's walk the sea shore,
        C                      G7
To see all the big ships as they sail o'er." Chorus
```

```
        C                                F
And while these two sisters were walking the

   shore,
        C                    F
Bow and balance to me.
        C                                F
And while these two sisters were walking the

   shore,
        C                            G7
The older one, she pushed the younger o'er. Chorus
```

```
        C                            F
"Oh sister, oh sister, please lend me your hand."
        C                  F
   Bow and balance to me.
        C                            F
"Oh sister, oh sister, please lend me your hand,
        C                          G7
Then you may have Willie and all of his land."
        Chorus
```

```
        C                        F
"I never, I never will lend you my hand."
        C                  F
   Bow and balance to me.
        C                        F
"I never, I never will lend you my hand,
        C                          G7
But I will have Willie and all of his land." Chorus
```

```
        C                         F
Sometimes she sank and sometimes she swam,
        C                 F
    Bow and balance to me.
        C                         F
Sometimes she sank and sometimes she swam,
        C                 G7
Until she came to the old mill dam. Chorus


            C                         F
"Oh father, oh father, come draw up your dam."
            C                 F
    Bow and balance to me.
            C                         F
"Oh father, oh father, come draw up your dam,
            C                 G7
Here's either a mermaid or a swan." Chorus


            C                 F
The miller, he got his fishing hook,
            C                 F
    Bow and balance to me.
            C                 F
The miller, he got his fishing hook,
            C                 G7
And fished the maiden out of the brook. Chorus
```

```
            C                         F
"Oh miller, oh miller, here's five gold rings."
            C                 F
    Bow and balance to me.
            C                         F
"Oh miller, oh miller, here's five gold rings,
            C                 G7
If you'll put me safe on shore again." Chorus


        C                         F
The miller received those five gold rings,
        C                 F
    Bow and balance to me.
        C                         F
The miller received those five gold rings,
        C                 G7
And pushed the maiden in again. Chorus


            C                         F
The miller was hung at his own mill gate,
            C                 F
    Bow and balance to me.
            C                         F
The miller was hung at his own mill gate,
            C                 G7
For drowning the youngest sister, Kate. Chorus
```

Since this pattern takes two measures to complete, if the chord change occurs in the second measure you have to decide whether or not you want to play the arpeggio in its customary place.

Rio Grande

Oh say, were you ev - er in

Rio - o Grande? Way, _____ oh, Ri - o. _____

_____ 'Tis there that the riv - er flows down gold - en sand. And we're

bound for the Ri - o Grande. Then, a - way,

boys,   a - way. _____   Way, _____   oh,

Ri - o. _____   So   fare — ye   well, —   my   pret - ty young

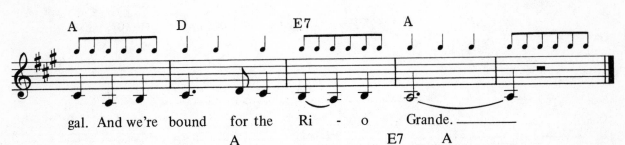

gal. And we're bound   for the   Ri - o   Grande. _____

                   A   E7   A
And goodbye, fare you well, all you ladies of town,

     Way, oh, Rio.
            D   A   E7   A
We've left you enough for to buy a silk gown,
              D   E7   A
And we're bound for the Rio Grande. *Chorus*

                  A   E7   A
It's pack up your donkey and get under way,

     Way, oh, Rio.
            D   A   E7   A
The girls we are leaving can take our half-pay,
              D   E7   A
And we're bound for the Rio Grande. *Chorus*

                  A   E7   A
Now, you Bowery ladies, we'd have you to know,

     Way, oh, Rio.
            D   A   E7   A
We're bound to the southward, Oh Lord, let us go,
              D   E7   A
And we're bound for the Rio Grande. *Chorus*

An all-arpeggio pattern.

At the Foot of Yonder Mountain

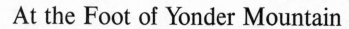

At the foot of yon - der moun - tain there

runs a clear stream, At the foot of yon - der moun - tain there

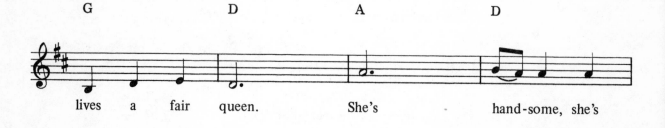

lives a fair queen. She's hand-some, she's

pro - per and her ways are com - plete. I_____

ask   no   oth-er pas-time than to be with my sweet.

      D   G   D
But why she won't have me I well understand:
                          G   D
She wants some freeholder and I have no land.
A D
I cannot maintain her on silver and gold,
                               G
And all the other fine things that my love's
                  D
house should hold.

      D   G   D
Oh, I wish I were a penman and could write a fine hand!
                                  G   D
I would write my love a letter from this distant land.
A D
I'd send it by the waters just for to let her know
                                  G   D
That I think of pretty Mary wherever I go.

      D   G   D
Oh, I wish I were a bird and had wings and could fly.
                                G   D
It's to my love's window this night I'd draw nigh.
A D
I'd sit in her window all night long and cry
                              G   D
That for love of pretty Mary I gladly would die.

Notice the two consecutive measures of arpeggios (measures 30-31). This was done to permit the last four measures of the song to begin with the chord-arpeggio sequence in its "proper" order.

Bill McCandless' Ride

Words and Music by
JERRY SILVERMAN

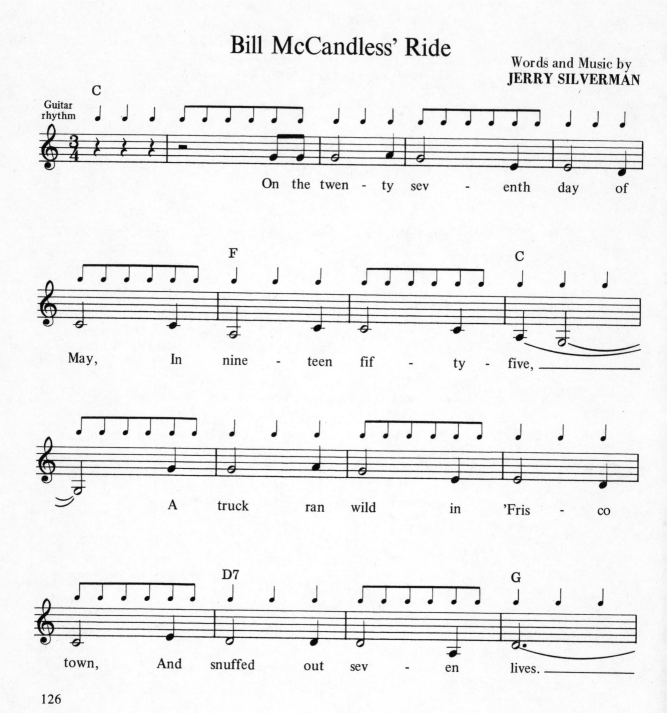

On the twen - ty sev - enth day of May, In nine - teen fif - ty - five, A truck ran wild in 'Fris - co town, And snuffed out sev - en lives.

126

Its air brakes failed on old Nob

Hill, As it was start - ing down, _____

And at one hun - dred miles an

Measure 30   *Measure 31*

watch out

hour _____ It tore through Chi - na -

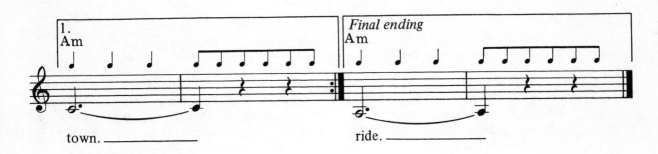

town. _____   ride. _____

Continued→

C
William R. McCandless,
    F   C
The driver of the van,

Stayed with it all down the hill,
    D7   G
And there died like a man.
        Am   D   Am
He called out to his helper then,
             C   G
Said, "Wayne, my brakes are gone.
        Am   D   C
You'd better jump and save yourself,
        Am   G   Am
For I can't hold on long."

      C
The truck picked up speed and then began
    F   C
McCandless' terrible ride.

He knew he was doomed, but to save other lives
    D7   G
He swerved from side to side.
       Am   D   Am
Pounding on a horn that was mute,
       C   G
He tried to stop the truck.
        Am   D
But he must have known as down he
   C
    roared
        Am   G   Am
That he would have no luck.

C
Clay Street was crowded with people that day,
    F   C
As the ten-ton truck sped down.

And when its awful course was run,
    D7   G
Six bodies lay on the ground.
      Am   D   Am
Then there came a terrible crash,
           C   G
As the van hit the front of a store.
         Am   D   C
When the police and fireman came they saw
      Am   G   Am
McCandless would drive no more.

     C
Take warning, all you drivers,
    F   C
Take warning in good time—

Remember Bill McCandless,
    D7   G
Who drove the Mayflower Line.
      Am   D   Am
Like Casey Jones he stuck to his post,
      C   G
And at his wheel he died,
        Am   D
And when songs of working heroes
   C
    are sung,
        Am   G   Am
We'll sing of McCandless' ride.

There is a new musical symbol in the following song: the **natural sign** ♮. This sign cancels a sharp or flat that may occur either in the key signature or as an accidental. Here the key signature of A major indicates three sharps—F sharp, C sharp and G sharp. However, the composer wanted a *G natural* in measure three of the chorus so the natural sign is used to cancel the G sharp. Two measures later the sharp sign appears in parenthesis in front of the note G. It was not absolutely necessary to write in a sharp sign here since the natural sign applies only in the measure where it occurs. The parenthetical sharp sign is just a reminder, that's all.

128

Overtures from Richmond

Words by
FRANCIS J. CHILD

Music "Liliburlero" by
HENRY PURCELL, c. 1686

Continued→

```
     A                    E7
"So, Uncle Sam, just lay down your arms."
     A    D6  E7       A
  Lilliburlero, old Uncle Sam.
                         E7
"Then you shall hear my reas'nable terms."
     A    D6  E7       A
  Lilliburlero, old Uncle Sam.
          C
"Lero, lero, I'd like to hear-o,
 D       E       A        E
I'd like to hear," says old Uncle Sam.
   D    A  E7   A
"Lero, lero, filibustero,
D maj 7   D6       E7        A
I'd like to hear," says old Uncle Sam.


     A                 E7
"First you must own I've beat you in fight."
     A    D6  E7       A
  Lilliburlero, old Uncle Sam.
                    E7
"Then that I always have been in the right."
     A    D6  E7       A
  Lilliburlero, old Uncle Sam.
          C
"Lero, lero, rather severe-o,
 D       E       A        E
Rather severe," says old Uncle Sam.
   D    A  E7   A
"Lero, lero, filibustero,
D maj 7   D6       E7        A
Rather severe," says old Uncle Sam.
```

```
     A                    E7
"Then you must pay me my national debts."
     A    D6  E7       A
  Lilliburlero, old Uncle Sam.
                    E7
"No questions asked about my assets."
     A    D6  E7       A
  Lilliburlero, old Uncle Sam.
          C
"Lero, lero, that's very dear-o,
 D       E       A        E
That's very dear," says old Uncle Sam.
   D    A  E7   A
"Lero, lero, filibustero,
D maj 7   D6       E7        A
That's very dear," says old Uncle Sam.


     A                    E7
"Next, you must own our Cavalier blood."
     A    D6  E7       A
  Lilliburlero, old Uncle Sam.
                         E7
"And that your Puritans sprang from the mud."
     A    D6  E7       A
  Lilliburlero, old Uncle Sam.
          C
"Lero, lero, that mud is clear-o,
 D       E       A        E
That mud is clear," says old Uncle Sam.
   D    A  E7   A
"Lero, lero, filibustero,
D maj 7   D6       E7        A
That mud is clear," says old Uncle Sam.
```

```
     A                 E7
"If to these terms you fully consent."
     A    D6  E7       A
  Lilliburlero, old Uncle Sam.
                    E7
"I'll be perpetual King-President."
     A    D6  E7       A
  Lilliburlero, old Uncle Sam.
             C
"Lero, lero, take your sombrero,
 D       E       A        E
Off to your swamps," says old Uncle Sam.
   D    A  E7   A
"Lero, lero, filibustero,
D maj 7       D6       E7        A
Cut, double quick," says old Uncle Sam.
```

Barre Chords

Chords where one finger covers more than one string are called **barre chords** (pronounced "bar"). We have already played a few chords where the index finger covered two or three strings. There is a very important group of chords for which the index finger must cover all six strings—like a capo. Then the remaining three fingers play certain other notes, depending on the chord.

Lay your index finger across all the strings

at the first fret. Keep the finger as stiff as possible and press down hard enough so that all six notes sound clearly. (This may take some doing.)

Keeping the barre firmly in place, play the pattern of an A chord with fingers two, three and four, two frets above the barre (just as you would play the A chord which is two frets above the nut). This is a B flat chord.

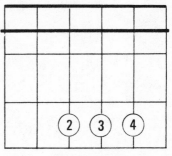

1st finger plays barre at 1st fret

B flat (B♭)

primary bass: 5
alternate bass: 6, 4

As I have just stated, it will take some doing to get all the notes to sound clearly, but it is definitely worth the effort not only for the sake of this B flat chord but because this pattern will give you a different major chord at every fret.

In other words, eleven chords for the price of one!

Barre on fret	Chord
1	B flat
2	B
3	C
4	C sharp (D flat)
5	D
6	D sharp (E flat)
7	E
8	F
9	F sharp (G flat)
10	G
11	G sharp (A flat)

You could keep going up (theoretically) to the 12th fret (an A chord), and beyond, but the chords repeat themselves from the 12th fret on. Also, it gets a little cramped up there.

Back to Arpeggios, Everybody!

With your new-found and future barre chords you will be able to play songs in any key with all the chords you need for rich, interesting harmonizations.

The six-beat arpeggio will show you whether or not you can play B flat properly.

The Great Silkie

Silkies are supernatural seal-folk who dwell in the depths of the sea near Sule Skerry and other Orkney and Hebrides islands off Scotland.

Words
TRADITIONAL

Music by
JERRY SILVERMAN

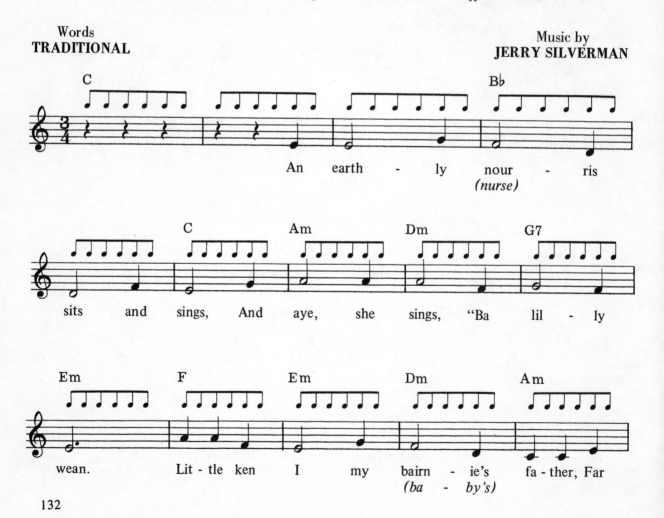

An earth - ly nour - ris
(nurse)
sits and sings, And aye, she sings, "Ba lil - ly
wean. Lit - tle ken I my bairn - ie's fa - ther, Far
(ba - by's)

less   the   land   that   he   sleeps   in. _____

      C   B♭   C
Then in he steps to her bedside,
        Am   Dm   G7   Em
And a grumbly guest I'm sure was he.
         F   Em   Dm   Am
Saying, "Here I am, thy bairnie's father,
      D   Am   B♭   C
Although I be not comely.

      C   B♭   C
"I am a man upon the land,
        Am   Dm   G7   Em
And I am a silkie in the sea.
         F   Em   Dm   Am
And when I'm far and far from land,
      D   Am   B♭   C
My home it is in Sule Skerry."

      C   B♭   C
Then he has taken a purse of gold,
      Am   Dm   G7   Em
And he has put it upon her knee.
          F   Em   Dm   Am
Saying, "Give to me my little young son,
      D   Am   B♭   C
And take thee up thy nourris fee.

       C   B♭   C
"It shall come to pass on a summer's day,
         Am   Dm   G7   Em
When the sun shines hot on every stone,
          F   Em   Dm   Am
That I shall take my little young son,
       D   Am   B♭   C
And teach him how to swim the foam.

       C   B♭   C
"And thou shall marry a proud gunner,
         Am   Dm   G7   Em
And a proud gunner, I'm sure he'll be.
          F   Em   Dm   Am
And the very first shot that e'er he'll shoot,
       D   Am   B♭   C
Will kill both my young son and me."

      C   B♭   C
"Alas, alas," the maiden cried,
        Am   Dm   G7   Em
This weary fate's been laid for me."
        F   Em   Dm   Am
And then she said, and then she said,
       D   Am   B♭   C
"I'll bury me in Sule Skerry."

133

Substitute a thumb beat for the second finger
in this six-beat arpeggio.

Scarborough Fair

Are you go - ing to Scar - bor-ough Fair?

Pars - ley sage, rose - ma - ry and thyme. Re -

mem - ber me to one who lives there,___ For

watch out

134

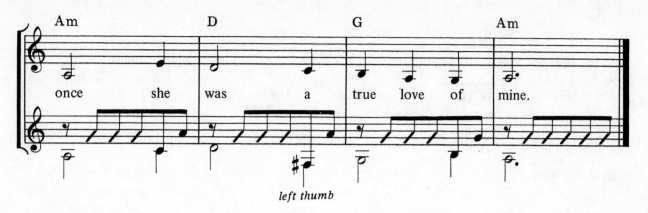

left thumb

Am   G Am
Tell her to make me a cambric shirt.
  C   Am D   Am
Parsley, sage, rosemary and thyme.
  F   C   G
Without any seam or fine needlework.
    Am   D G   Am
And then she'll be a true love of mine.

Am   G Am
Tell her to wash it in yonder dry well.
  C   Am D   Am
Parsley, sage, rosemary and thyme.
    F   C
Where water ne'er sprung, nor drop of rain
  G
  fell.
    Am   D G   Am
And then she'll be a true love of mine.

Am   G Am
Tell her to dry it on yonder thorn.
  C   Am D   Am
Parsley, sage, rosemary and thyme.
    F   C
Which never bore blossom since Adam was
    G
  born.
    Am   D G   Am
And then she'll be a true love of mine.

Am   G   Am
Will you find me an acre of land.
  C   Am D   Am
Parsley, sage, rosemary and thyme.
  F   C   G
Between the sea foam and the sea sand.
  Am D G   Am
Or never be a true love of mine.

Am   G   Am
Will you plough it with a lamb's horn.
  C   Am D   Am
Parsley, sage, rosemary and thyme.
  F   C   G
And sow it all over with one peppercorn,
  Am D G   Am
Or never be a true love of mine.

Am   G   Am
Will you reap it with sickle of leather.
  C   Am D   Am
Parsley, sage, rosemary and thyme.
  F   C   G
And tie it all up with a peacock's feather.
  Am D G   Am
Or never be a true love of mine.

Am   G   Am
When you've done and finished your work.
  C   Am D   Am
Parsley, sage, rosemary and thyme.
  F   C   G
Then come to me for your cambric shirt.
  Am D G   Am
And you shall be a true love of mine.

Six-Eight Time ($\frac{6}{8}$)

Another common metrical arrangement of notes within a measure is six eight-note beats. In $\frac{6}{8}$ time the unit of counting is the eighth note and there are six eighth notes (or their equivalent) per measure.

The basic bass-chord strum in $\frac{6}{8}$ is somewhat similar *physically* to $\frac{2}{4}$. *Musically*, however, it is quite another matter.

- Finger a C chord.
- Count slowly and evenly: 1 2 3 4 5 6, 1 2 3 4 5 6, 1 2 3 4 5 6 . . .
- Play bass on 1.
- Chord up-pluck on 3.
- Bass on 4.
- Up-pluck on 6.
- Go back to 1 and repeat.
- *Do not pause between 3 and 4, 6 and 1.*

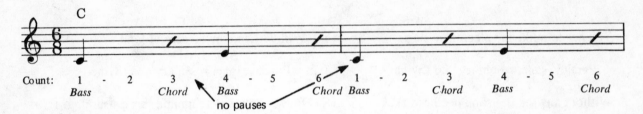

The rhythm of the melody of *Rig a Jig Jig* is, for the most part, identical with the strum.

In the few places where the melody changes rhythm *keep the strum going*.

Rig a Jig Jig

As I was walk - ing down the street,

down the street, down the street, As I was walk - ing down the street, Hi -

Chorus:

ho, hi - ho, hi - ho. _____ Rig a jig jig, and a - way we go, A -

136

way   we   go,   A - way   we   go.   Rig   a   jig   jig,   and   a -

way   we   go,   Hi - ho,   hi - ho,   hi - ho.

            A
A pretty girl I chanced to meet,
  E7   A
Chanced to meet, chanced to meet.

A pretty girl I chanced to meet,
    E7   A
Hi-ho, hi-ho, hi-ho. *Chorus*

        A
I asked her would she walk with me,
  E7   A
Walk with me, walk with me.

I asked her would she walk with me,
    E7   A
Hi-ho, hi-ho, hi-ho. *Chorus*

        A
She said, "Kind sir, I'll walk with ye,
  E7   A
Walk with ye, walk with ye."

She said, "Kind sir, I'll walk with ye."
    E7   A
Hi-ho, hi-ho, hi-ho. *Chorus*

        A
We strolled together merrily,
  E7   A
Merrily, merrily.

We strolled together merrily,
    E7   A
Hi-ho, hi-ho, hi-ho. *Chorus*

There are three new barre chords in *The Lincolnshire Poacher*.

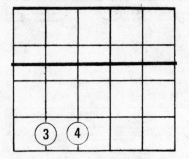

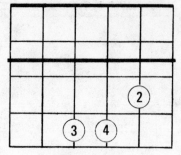

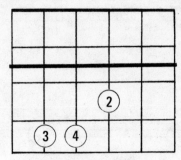

F sharp minor (F♯m)
primary bass: 6
alternate bass: 5, 4
Relationship to D: III

B minor
primary bass: 5
alternate bass: 6, 4
Relationship to D: VI

F sharp (F♯)
primary bass: 6
alternate bass: 5, 4
Relationship to D:
III major, or
V of VI (Bm)

As with the B flat chord, you can play these patterns at any fret and get the following other chords:

Fret	Chord	Chord
1	B♭m	F (minor or major)
2	Bm	F♯ (G♭)
3	Cm	G
4	C♯m (D♭m)	G♯ (A♭)
5	Dm	A
6	D♯m (E♭m)	B♭
7	Em	B
8	Fm	C
9	F♯m (G♭m)	C♯ (D♭)
10	Gm	D
11	G♯m (A♭m)	D♯ (E♭)

The Lincolnshire Poacher

Chords in brackets
may be omitted

When I was bound ap - pren - tice in

fa - mous Lin - coln - shire, Full well I served my mas - ter for

138

more than sev - en year,___ Un - til I took to poach - ing, as

Chorus:

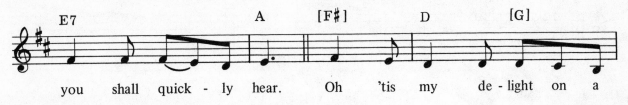

you shall quick - ly hear. Oh 'tis my de - light on a

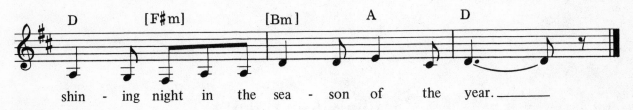

shin - ing night in the sea - son of the year._____

      D   [G]   D [F♯m] [Bm]
As me and my companions were a-setting
     A   D
    of a snare,
               [F♯m] [Bm]
'Twas then we spied the gamekeeper,
     E7   A
    for him we did not care.
    D   [F♯m] [Bm]
For we can wrestle and fight, my boys,
     E7   A
    and jump out anywhere. *Chorus*

      D   [G]   D [F♯m] [Bm]
As me and my companions were a-setting
     A   D
    four or five,
           [F♯m] [Bm] E7
And taking them up once again, we caught
     A
    a hare alive.
    D   [F♯m]   [Bm]
We took a hare alive, my boys,
     E7   A
    and through the woods did steer. *Chorus*

      D   [G]   D [F♯m] [Bm]
I threw him on my shoulder and then we
     A   D
    trug-ed home.
             [F♯m]   [Bm]   E7
We took him to a neighbor's house and sold
          A
    him for a crown.
    D   [F♯m]   [Bm]
We sold him for a crown, my boys,
     E7   A
    but I won't tell you where. *Chorus*

      D   [G] D [F♯m]   [Bm]
Success to every gentleman that lives in
     A   D
    Lincolnshire.
            [F♯m] [Bm] E7
Success to every poacher that wants to sell
     A
    a hare.
    D   [F♯m] [Bm]   E7
Bad luck to every gamekeeper, of them
          A
    we have no fear. *Chorus*

Arpeggios in ⁶⁄₈ Time

We subdivide the second half of the basic strum into three eighth notes. Follow the fingering and keep counting evenly to six.

Right hand	T		F	T	1	2	T		F	T	1	2
Count:	1 - 2		3	4	5	6	1 - 2		3	4	5	6

Hullabaloo Belay

Me moth - er kept a board - ing house,

Hul - la - ba - loo be - lay,   Hul - la - ba - loo ba - la be - lay, And

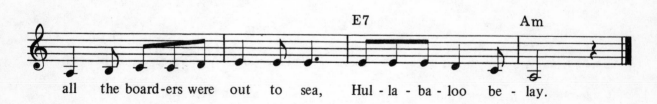

all the board-ers were out to sea,   Hul - la - ba - loo be - lay.

Am
A fresh young fellow named Shallo Brown,

   Hullabaloo belay,

   Hullabaloo, bala, belay,

He followed me mother all 'round the town,
  E7   Am
  Hullabaloo belay.

     Am
Me father said, "Look here, me boy!"

   Hullabaloo belay,

   Hullabaloo, bala, belay.

To which he quickly made reply,
    E7   Am
  "Hullabaloo belay."

     Am
One day when father was in the Crown,

   Hullabaloo belay,

   Hullabaloo, bala, belay,

Me mother ran off with Shallo Brown,
  E7   Am
  Hullabaloo belay.

     Am
Me father slowly pined away,

   Hullabaloo belay,

   Hullabaloo, bala, belay,

'Cause mother came back the very next day,
  E7   Am
  Hullabaloo belay.

When the chord changes in the middle of
the measure, keep the arpeggio pattern going.

Fillimeeoriay

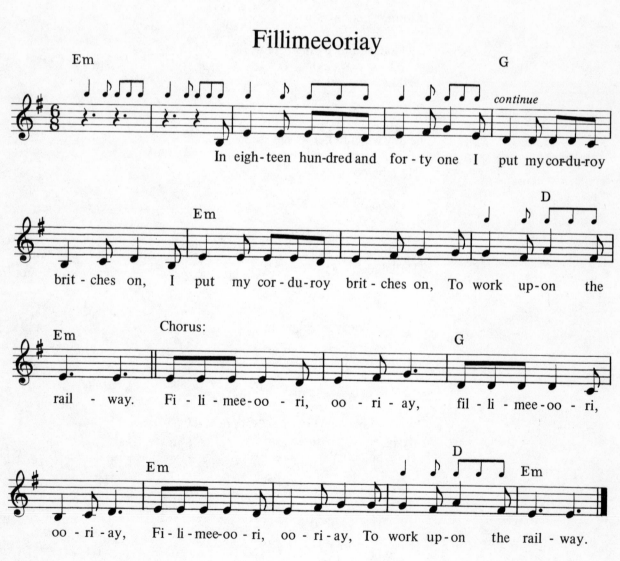

In eigh-teen hun-dred and for-ty one I put my cor-du-roy

brit-ches on, I put my cor-du-roy brit-ches on, To work up-on the

Chorus:

rail-way. Fi - li - mee-oo - ri, oo - ri - ay, fil - li - mee-oo - ri,

oo - ri - ay, Fi - li - mee-oo - ri, oo - ri - ay, To work up-on the rail - way.

Em
In eighteen hundred and forty-two,
　G
I left the old world for the new,
　Em
I left the old world for the new,
　　　D　　Em
To work upon the railway. *Chorus*

　Em
In eighteen hundred and forty-three,
　　G
'Twas then I met sweet Biddy McGee.
　Em
An elegant wife she's been to me,
　　　D　　Em
While working on the railway. *Chorus*

　Em
In eighteen hundred and forty-four,
　　G
We worked again and worked some more.
　　Em
It's, "Bend your backs!" the boss did roar,
　　　D　　Em
While working on the railway. *Chorus*

Em
In eighteen hundred and forty-five,
　G
They worked us just like bees in a hive.
　Em
I didn't know if I was dead or alive,
　　　D　　Em
While working on the railway. *Chorus*

　Em
In eighteen hundred and forty-six,
　　G
They pelted me with stones and sticks.
　　Em
Sure, I was in a terrible fix,
　　　D　　Em
While working on the railway. *Chorus*

　Em
In eighteen hundred and forty-seven,
　　G
Sweet Biddy McGee, she went to heaven.
　　Em
If she left one child, she left eleven,
　　　D　　Em
To work upon the railway. *Chorus*

The Darby Ram

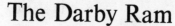

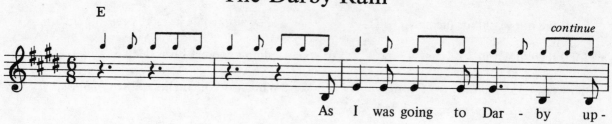

As I was going to Dar - by up -

on a mar - ket day, ___ I saw the big - gest ram, sir, That

optional bass run

ev - er was fed on hay, ___ That ev - er was fed on hay.

E
The ram was fat behind, sir,
               B7   E
The ram was fat before.
    F♯m   B7
He measured ten yards round, sir,
    A   B7   E
I think it was no more. *(Repeat)*

        E
And he who knocked this ram down,
               B7   E
Was drown-ed in the blood.
    F♯m   B7
And he who held the dish, sir,
    A   B7   E
Was carried away by the flood. *(Repeat)*

E
The wool grew on his back, sir,
      B7   E
It reached up to the sky.
  F♯m   B7
The eagles built their nests there,
  A   B7   E
I heard the young ones cry. *(Repeat)*

E
And all the boys in Darby, sir,
       B7   E
Came begging for his eyes,
  F♯m   B7
To knock about the street, sir,
  A   B7   E
As any good football flies. *(Repeat)*

E
The horns upon his head, sir,
      B7   E
Were high as man could reach.
  F♯m   B7
And there they built a pulpit, sir,
  A   B7   E
The Quakers for to preach. *(Repeat)*

E
And one of this ram's teeth, sir,
      B7   E
Was hollow as a horn.
  F♯m   B7
And when they took its measure, sir,
  A   B7   E
It held a bushel of corn. *(Repeat)*

E
The mutton that this ram made,
      B7   E
Gave the whole army meat.
  F♯m   B7
And what was left, I'm told, sir,
  A   B7   E
Was served out to the fleet. *(Repeat)*

E
The man who owned this ram, sir,
       B7   E
Was considered mighty rich.
    F♯m   B7
But the man who told this story, sir,
  A   B7   E
Was a lying son of a bitch. *(Repeat)*

Johnny Is My Darling

Johnny is my darling, my darling, my

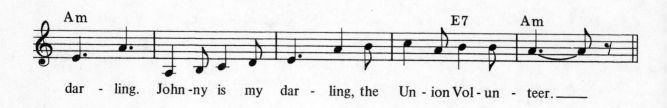

darling. Johnny is my darling, the Union Volunteer.____

Verse:

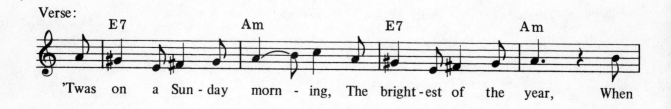

'Twas on a Sunday morning, The brightest of the year, When

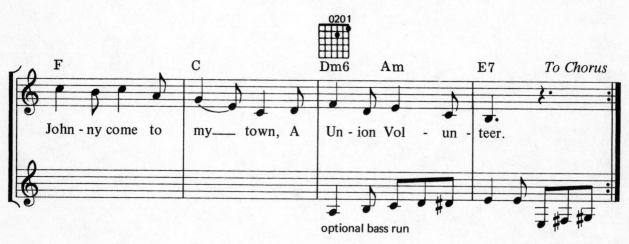

Johnny come to my____ town, A Union Volunteer.

optional bass run

146

```
      E7                     Am
As he came marching up the street,
      E7                        Am
The bands played loud and clear.
      F              C
And everyone came out to greet
      Dm6    Am   E7
The Union Volunteer. Chorus


      E7                 Am
With proudly waving starry flags,
      E7                  Am
And heart that knew no fear;
      F              C
He came to fight for Freedom's rights,
      Dm6     Am E7
A Union Volunteer. Chorus


      E7                      Am
But though he's gone to glory win,
      E7            Am
And I left lonely here,
      F                C
He'll soon return to me again
      Dm6    Am    E7
As Cupid's Volunteer. Chorus
```

In the following all-arpeggio pattern be sure to give the fourth note (played by the third finger) a strong accent.

If the chord changes in the middle of the measure, we play two groups of three.

Gently, Johnny, My Jingalo

I put my hand all in her own.

Fair maid is a lil - y, O. She said, "If you love me a - lone,

Chorus:

Come to me qui - et - ly, Do not do me in - ju - ry;

guitar counterpoint - for a change

Gen - tly, John - ny, my Jin - ga - lo."

Guitar interlude

D   C   D
I said, "You know I love you, dear."
    G   A7 D
Fair maid is a lily, O.
          C   D
She whispered softly in my ear. *Chorus*

D   C   D
I kissed her lips like rubies red.
    G   A7 D
Fair maid is a lily, O.
          C   D
She blushed, then tenderly she said. *Chorus*

D   C   D
I placed my arm around her waist.
    G   A7 D
Fair maid is a lily, O.
          C   D
She laughed and turned away her face. *Chorus*

D   C   D
I slipped a ring all in her hand.
    G   A7 D
Fair maid is a lily, O.
          C   D
She said, "The parson's near at hand." *Chorus*

      D   C   D
I took her to the church next day.
        G   A7 D
Fair maid is a lily, O.
            C   D
The birds did sing and she did say. *Chorus*

4
COUNTRY and BLUEGRASS GUITAR

Instrumental technique is a cumulative process. The chords, strums, arpeggios and runs that you have learned up to this point apply not only to the songs in the preceding chapters but to much of the music yet to be covered.

The ability to read melodies—so useful for learning new songs—should also be put to the test in this and succeeding chapters.

Hammering-On

- Finger a C chord.

- While keeping the third and first fingers in place lift the second finger off its note (E), exposing the open D string.

- Play D with your thumb.

- While the note D is sounding return the raised second finger to the second fret of the D string. Hit the string hard with that finger. The note E should sound.

- You have just hammered-on.

- Now pluck the first three strings of the the C chord in the normal right hand manner.

hammer-on   up-pluck

We can make a four-beat strum out of this by placing a bass chord before the hammer-on.

Observe that the two notes of the hammer-on are eighth notes. Don't rush them.

Count: 1   2   3 - and   4   1   2   3 - and   4

150

Try similar strums with F and G7.

Thumb plays *watch out*
3rd string

If we subdivide the last beat of this strum
into a two-note arpeggio we have the following:

watch out

watch out   *watch out*

After you have played *Going Down the Road* with this pattern and feel fairly comfortable with it, add bass runs in their customary places. In the measures where the bass runs are played they take the place of the hammer-on arpeggio.

Going Down the Road Feeling Bad

I'm go-ing down the road feel-ing bad,—

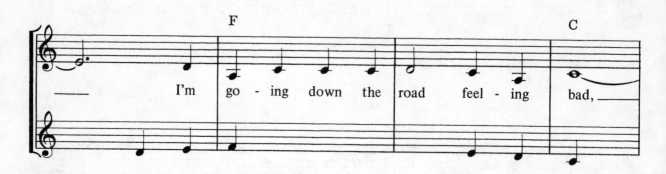

— I'm go - ing down the road feel - ing bad,—

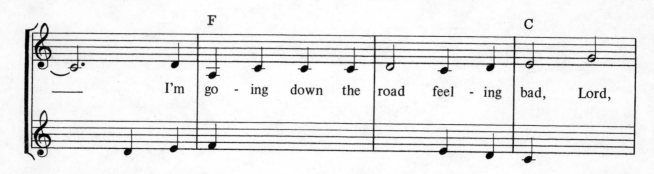

— I'm go - ing down the road feel - ing bad, Lord,

Lord,— And I ain't gon-na be treat-ed this - a - way.—

C
Two-dollar shoes hurt my feet,
 F   C
Two-dollar shoes hurt my feet,
 F   C
Two-dollar shoes hurt my feet, Lord, Lord,
      G7   C
And I ain't gonna be treated this-a-way.

 C
Ten-dollar shoes suit me fine,
 F   C
Ten-dollar shoes suit me fine,
 F   C
Ten-dollar shoes suit me fine, Lord, Lord,
      G7   C
And I ain't gonna be treated this-a-way.

       C
I'm down in the jail on my knees,
      F   C
I'm down in the jail on my knees,
      F   C
I'm down in the jail on my knees, Lord, Lord,
      G7   C
And I ain't gonna be treated this-a-way.

       C
They fed me on cornbread and peas,
      F   C
They fed me on cornbread and peas,
      F   C
They fed me on cornbread and peas, Lord, Lord,
      G7   C
And I ain't gonna be treated this-a-way.

          C
I'm going where the water tastes like wine,
      F   C
I'm going where the water tastes like wine,
      F   C
I'm going where the water tastes like wine, Lord, Lord,
           G7   C
'Cause this prison water tastes like turpentine.

Repeat first verse

For *Wildwood Flower,* the hammer-on on the G chord is the same as for the G7. We ordinarily do not hammer-on the D7. Just play the regular bass-chord arpeggio when you come to D7.

Wildwood Flower

```
       G                        D7        G
Oh, he promised to love me, he promised  to love
                    D7        G
And to cherish me over all others above.
                              C        G
I woke from my dream and my idol was clay,
                    D7     G
My passion for loving had vanished away.


         G                        D7        G
Oh, he taught me to love him, he called me his flower,
                         D7        G
A blossom to cheer him through life's weary  hour.
                    C        G
But now he is gone and left me alone,
                         D7        G
The wild flowers to weep and the wild birds to mourn.


      G                        D7        G
I'll dance and I'll sing and my life shall be gay.
                         D7        G
I'll charm every heart in the crowd I survey.
                              C        G
Though my heart now is breaking, he never shall know
                              D7
How his name makes me tremble, my pale
            G
      cheeks to glow.


         G                        D7        G
I'll dance and I'll sing and my heart will be gay.
                         D7        G
I'll banish this weeping, drive troubles away.
                    C        G
I'll live yet to see him regret this dark hour,
                         D7           G
When he won and neglected his frail wildwood  flower.
```

The Church Lick

- Finger an A chord.
- Play the bass note (A) with your thumb.
- Brush down with your fingernails over the rest of the chord (primarily strings 1, 2, 3).
- Brush up lightly with your index finger over the first two or three strings.
- Follow the rhythm carefully.

After you have played *Roll on the Ground* with the church lick and feel fairly comfortable with it, add bass runs in their customary places.

There are two church licks per measure. The bass run takes the place of the second church lick.

Roll on the Ground

```
      A
Work on the railroad,
 D        A
Dollar a day.
 D        A
Eat soda crackers,
   E7         A
Wind blow'm away. Chorus


      A
Big ball's in Nashville,
 D          A
Big ball in town.
 D        A
Eat soda crackers,
   E7         A
Roll on the ground. Chorus


      A
Goin' up to Nashville,
 D          A
Have me a time.
 D        A
Eat soda crackers,
   E7      A
Ten for a dime. Chorus
```

The church lick may be combined with the hammer-on, depending on the chords involved. The hammer-on comes at its customary place —the third beat. The up and down strokes of the church lick are not affected by this since they occur on the second and fourth beats.

Don't forget the bass runs.

Nine-Pound Hammer

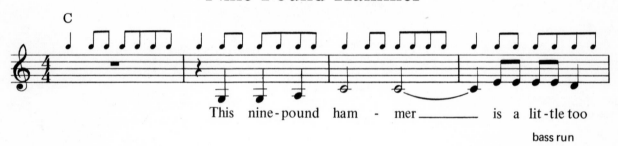

This nine-pound ham - mer _____ is a lit-tle too

bass run

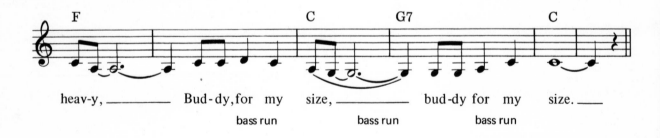

heav-y, _____ Bud-dy, for my size, _____ bud-dy for my size. _____

bass run   bass run   bass run

Chorus:

Roll on, bud -dy, _____ pull a load_ of coal. _____ How can I
bud -dy, _____ don't you pull_ so slow. _____ How can I

bass run   bass run

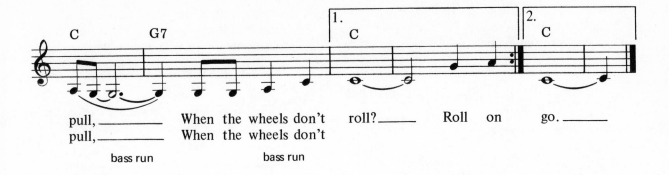

pull, ———— When the wheels don't roll?——— Roll on go. ———
pull, ———— When the wheels don't

bass run   bass run

C
It's a long way to Harlan,
     F
It's a long way to Hazard,
      C G7
Just to get a little brew,
       C
Just to get a little brew. *Chorus*

C
Ain't nobody's hammer
      F
On this mountain,
      C G7
Rings like mine,
      C
Rings like mine. *Chorus*

C
Went up on the mountain,
      F
Just to see my sweet thing.
       C G7
And I ain't coming back,
       C
No, I ain't coming back. *Chorus*

159

The Extended Church Lick

- Finger an E chord.
- Play the bass note (E).
- Brush down with your fingernails (but not up again).
- Play the bass note.

- Brush *up* with your index finger.
- Brush down and up in the good old church lick manner.
- Follow the rhythm and the various up and down strokes very carefully.

Mule Skinner Blues

Well it's, good morn - ing,

cap - tain, ___ Good morn - ing, son, ___ And it's,

good morn - ing, cap - tain. ___ Good morn - ing, son.

160

watch out

E   E7
Well, I like to work, I'm rolling all the time,
     A   E
And I like to work, I'm rolling all the time.
     B7   E
I can pop my initials right on a mule's behind.

          E   E7
Well it's, hey little water boy, bring your water 'round,
          A   E
And it's, hey little water boy, bring your water 'round.
     B7   E
If you don't like your job, set that water bucket down.

          E   E7
I'm a-working on that new road at a dollar and a dime a day,
          A   E
I'm a-working on that new road at a dollar and a dime a day,
          B7   E
I've got three women waiting on a Saturday night just to draw my pay.

The Blues Wrinkle

The action of the **blues wrinkle** takes place on the fourth beat (down-up) of the extended church lick. On that last downstroke, while playing an E chord lift the first finger off its note (G sharp). The open G string will then sound. On the following up-stroke replace the first finger (don't hammer-on). The G sharp will sound again.

The alternation of G sharp and G (or E major and E minor chords) gives a very definite blues feeling.

To get the same pattern with the A chord you must finger it this way:

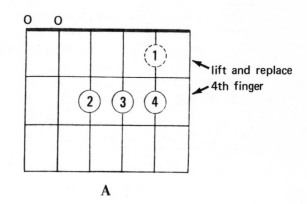

A

For B7 we change the pattern somewhat, hammering-on with the first finger on the third beat.

Hammer-on

Try *Mule Skinner Blues* this way. Other songs in E that you have played, especially *Crawdad* and *This Train,* will sound very good with the extended church lick and the blues wrinkle.

A Snappy Ending

Ending a song other than by just stopping is of great importance—particularly in country and bluegrass music where instrumental technique is highly valued.

There is one run or **break** that is often played to signal "the end." It begins on the first beat of the last measure. In C it goes like this. Watch for the double hammer-on and the **pull-off**. For the pull-off, the left hand "flicks," or pulls away from its note to play a lower note.

You can play *Tom Dooley* with the hammering-on arpeggio strum *or* the church lick—hammer-on (or both, as you like it). Bass runs, too!

Hang Down Your Head, Tom Dooley

Hang down your head, Tom Doo-ley, Hang down your head and cry.

Hang down your head, Tom Doo-ley, Poor boy, you're bound to die.

C
You took her on the hillside
                     G7
To make her be your wife.

You took her on the hillside,
                        C
And there you took her life.

          C
Take down my old fiddle
                    G7
And play it all you please.

At this time tomorrow
                  C
It'll be no use to me.

          C
This time tomorrow,
               G7
Reckon where I'll be?

If it hadn't been for Grayson,
                     C
I'd a-been in Tennessee.

          C
This time tomorrow,
               G7
Reckon where I'll be?

Down in some lonesome valley,
                     C
Hanging from a big oak tree.

Repeat first verse

Here's an ending in G.

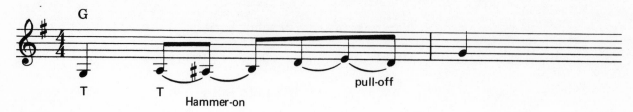

T   T   T
Hammer-on   pull-off

Bass runs between G and E minor.

Hammer-on in E minor.

Church lick, arpeggio, hammer-on, bass
runs, snappy endings . . . Do your thing!

Bowling Green

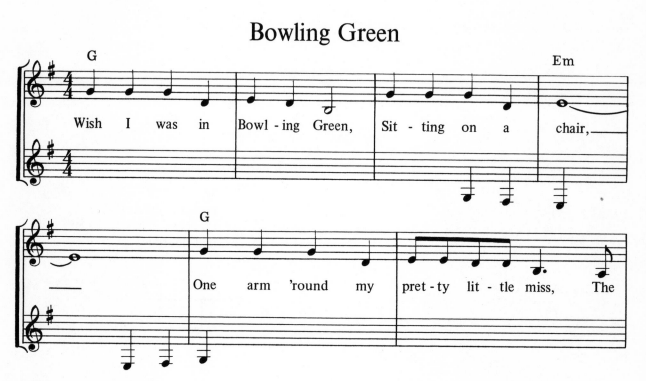

Wish I was in Bowl-ing Green, Sit-ting on a chair,

One arm 'round my pret-ty lit-tle miss, The

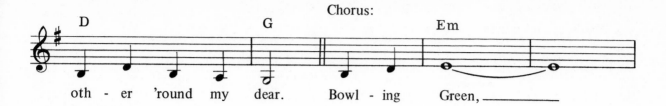

oth - er 'round my dear. Bowl - ing Green, _____

Chorus:

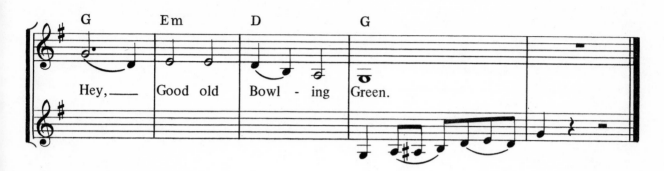

Hey, _____ Good old Bowl - ing Green.

G
If you see that gal of mine,
   Em
Tell her once for me:
G
If she loves another man,
D   **G**
Yes, I'll set her free. *Chorus*

G
Wish I was a bumblebee,
    Em
Sailing through the air.
G
Sail right down to my gal's side,
D   **G**
Touch her if you dare. *Chorus*

   G
Going through this whole wide world,
     Em
Going through alone.
 G
Going through this whole wide world,
D   **G**
I ain't got no home. *Chorus*

Pick a Number

- Finger a D chord.

- Play a simple church lick (bass down-up).

- Follow the music carefully for the next four eighth notes. This pattern is sometimes called **double-thumbing.**

Right hand T 1 1 T 2 T 1 T 1 1 T 2 T 1

Watch out for the runs from D to B7 to E minor to A7 in *Buddy, Won't You Roll Down the Line?* Try A7 this way.

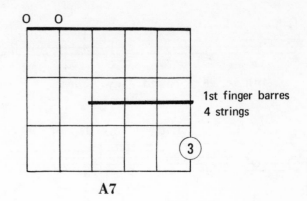

1st finger barres
4 strings

A7

Buddy, Won't You Roll Down the Line?

Way back yon-der in Ten-nes-see, they leased the con-victs

out.   Put them work-ing in the mines, A-gainst free la-bor,

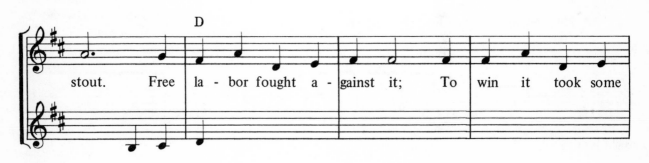

stout.   Free la-bor fought a-gainst it;   To win it took some

168

time, But while the lease was in ef-fect, They made 'em rise and shine.

Chorus:

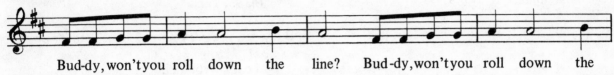

Bud-dy, won't you roll down the line? Bud-dy, won't you roll down the

line? Yon - der comes my dar - ling, com - ing down the

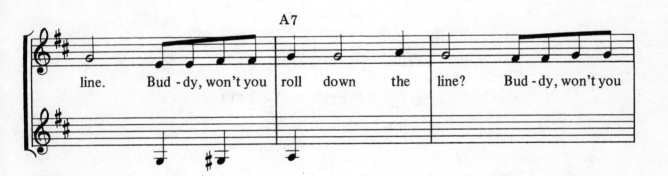

line. Bud - dy, won't you roll down the line? Bud - dy, won't you

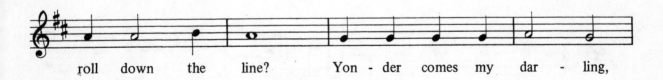

roll down the line? Yon - der comes my dar - ling,

com - ing down the line. Guitar - - - - - - - - - - - - - 3/4 - - - -

Continued→

D
Early Monday morning they get you up

on time,
A7
Send you down to Lone Rock just to look into

that mine.
D
Send you down to Lone Rock to look into

that hole,
A7
Very next thing the captain says, "You better
                    D
get your pole." *Chorus*

D
The beans they are half-done, the bread is not

so well,
A7
The meat, it is all burnt up, and the coffee's

black as hell.
D
But when you get your task done, and it's on

the floor you fall,
A7
Anything you get to eat would taste good, done
                    D
or raw. *Chorus*

D
The bank boss, he's a hard man, a man you all

know well,
A7
And if you don't get your task done, he's gonna

give you hell.
D
Carry you to the stockade, and it's on the floor

you fall.
A7
Very next word that you hear, "You better get
                    D
your pole." *Chorus*

Since E uses all six strings you have some
more choices for double-thumbing. Make some
patterns up yourself, also.

Don't forget the bass runs!

170

Bury Me Beneath the Willow

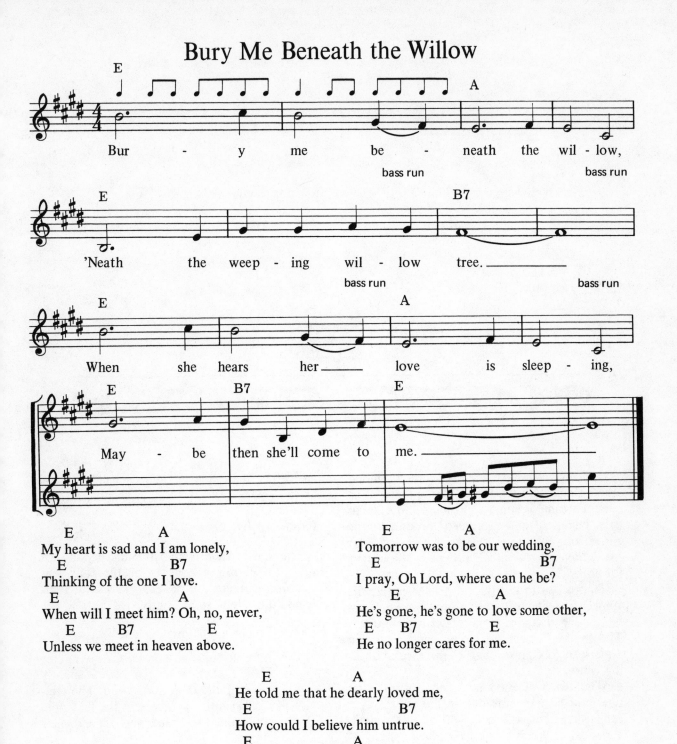

My heart is sad and I am lonely,
Thinking of the one I love.
When will I meet him? Oh, no, never,
Unless we meet in heaven above.

Tomorrow was to be our wedding,
I pray, Oh Lord, where can he be?
He's gone, he's gone to love some other,
He no longer cares for me.

He told me that he dearly loved me,
How could I believe him untrue.
Until one day some neighbors told me,
"He has proven untrue to you."

Repeat first verse

171

5

GOSPEL GUITAR

Up to now we have been concerned, among other things, with rhythmic continuity. That is, once a strum or some right-hand pattern has been begun, it has continued throughout the entire song. While this approach is valid for many areas of folk music it does not hold true for all.

That is not to say that in gospel guitar, the subject under consideration here, we shall not be playing rhythmic strums. On the contrary: The rhythmic element is nowhere stronger in American folk music than in this vital, pulsating genre.

What we will encounter here for the first time will be moments during the course of a song when the basic beat will be interrupted. Paradoxically, this break will serve to strength-en, rather than weaken, the overall rhythmic drive.

Rocking Rhythm

The basic underlying rhythmic feeling of most gospel music consists of the four-beat measure, with each of the beats subdivided unevenly into "long-short" units.

- Finger a C chord.

- Play just the bass note, C, giving the first of each group of two a slightly longer pulse than the second. The feeling is similar to $\frac{6}{8}$, where the first note gets "one-two" and the second gets "three."

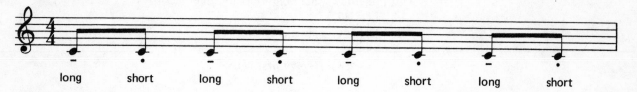

| long | short | long | short | long | short | long | short |

172

Now play two successive bass notes and two successive chordal up-plucks in this rhythm.

This can be varied.

Try it with a barre F chord.

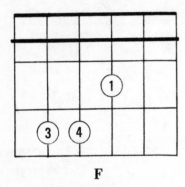

F

primary bass: 6
alternate bass: 5, 4

This is a particularly useful barre chord formation. We've seen it before. Remember what you get from it?

Fret	Chord
1	F
2	F♯ (G♭)
3	G
4	G♯ (A♭)
5	A
6	B♭
7	B
8	C
9	C♯ (D♭)
10	D
11	E♭

When you switch back and forth from C to barre F the third finger does not move.

This rocking strum works very well for *Walk Jerusalem,* except for the last measure of the chorus and verse. Here is where we must interrupt it and play something else.

For emphasis on the words "just like John" we pluck bass and C, F, C chords *together*—one quarter-note beat for each chord. The fourth beat is a rest so don't play anything. Then begin the strum again with the first beat of the next measure.

Walk in Jerusalem

174

meet me there. Walk in Je - ru - sa - lem, — just like John.

          C
Oh, John, oh, John, what do you say?
       F   C F C
Walk in Jerusalem, just like John.
                   E7   Am
That I'll be there in the coming day.
       F   C F C
Walk in Jerusalem, just like John. *Chorus*

          C
When Peter was preaching at Pentacost.
       F   C F C
Walk in Jerusalem, just like John.
                   E7   Am
He was endowed with the Holy Ghost.
       F   C F C
Walk in Jerusalem, just like John. *Chorus*

The usual bass runs can be adapted to this rhythm.

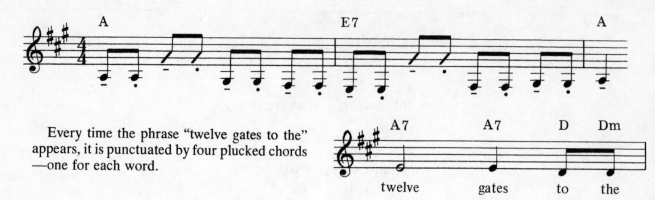

Every time the phrase "twelve gates to the" appears, it is punctuated by four plucked chords —one for each word.

The word **tacet** means do not play. In this song it is preceded by sharply struck (with the thumb) A chords. The symbol > means that a

chord or note is to be played with particular emphasis.

Twelve Gates to the City

A Tacet   **A Tacet**   **A Tacet**

Three gates in the east,   Three gates in the west,   Three gates in the north,

Guitar

Last time, D.C. al Fine

A Tacet   **A7**   **A7**   **D Dm A**   **E7**   **A D**   **A**

Three gates in the south. There's twelve gates to the ci-ty, hal-le-lu-jah.

Means Da Capo *(from the beginning) to the measure marked* Fine *(pron. "feenay") — the end.*

Verse:

A   **A7**   **A7**   **D Dm**

Who are these chil-dren there, dressed in red? There's twelve gates to the
must be the chil-dren that Mo - ses led.

D   **D**   **Bb7**   **Bb7**

day,   ev - 'ry day,   ev - 'ry

A   **E7**   **A D**   **1. A**   **2. A**

ci - ty, hal - le - lu - jah.   It   jah.

       A
When I get to heaven, gonna sing and shout,
      A7   A7 D Dm A   E7 A D A
There's twelve gates to the city hallelu-u-jah.
      A
Ain't nobody there gonna put me out,
      A7   A7 D Dm A
There's twelve gates to the city,
     E7 A D A
hallelu-u-jah. *Chorus*

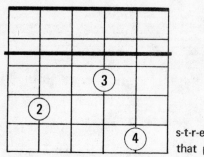

F#7
primary bass: 6
alternate bass: 5
Relationship to D: III7 major, or
V7 of VI (Bm)

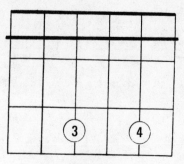

Bb7
primary bass: 5
alternate bass: 6, 4
Relationship to D: bVI7 major

s-t-r-e-t-c-h
that pinky!

Check the chord tables for F-sharp minor and B-flat major to see what other chords you can get from these two. They will have the same letters of alphabet but will, of course, be "sevenths."

A number of new runs have been written into this arrangement. They are all to be played

in the rocking rhythm. Also, watch out for a "new" E7 in the next to last measure.

The "ev'ry day" part gives us our rhythmic break. The D and B flat 7 are played only on the second and third beats of their respective measures.

This Little Light of Mine

This lit - tle light of mine, I'm gon - na let it shine,

This lit - tle light of mine, I'm gon - na let it shine,

This lit - tle light of mine, I'm gon - na let it shine. Ev -'ry

178

day,   ev-'ry day,   ev-'ry day, ev - 'ry   day,___ Gon-na

let   my   lit - tle light   shine._____

On   Mon -day He gave me the   gift   of   love, On Tues-day peace came

from a - bove. On We'n's-day He gave me a   lit - tle more faith, On

Thurs-day gave   me   a   lit - tle more grace. On Fri -day He told me just

what to   say,   On Sat - ur -day, told me to   watch and pray.   On

D.C. al Fine

Sun-day gave me   pow-er di - vine, Just to   let   my   lit -tle light shine. Oh!

179

The Subdominant Switcheroo

A harmonic characteristic of many gospel songs is a very strong feeling for the subdominant—the IV chord. In order to be able to switch back and forth endlessly between C and its subdominant, F, anchor your third and first fingers in place on the C chord and then play F like this. With your thumb and fingers of your right hand pluck only strings 5, 4, 3, and 2. No first string for either C or F.

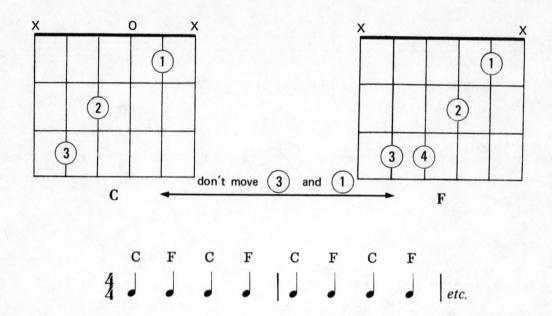

For the chorus of *Let Me Fly*, we revert back to the simple basic thumb-chord strum except in the two measures where the guitar echoes the voice.

On the last "Lord" of the chorus C–F alternation begins again, leading into the next verse. At the end of the final chorus just play "C F C F C," as written and stop on the last C.

Let Me Fly

Way down yon-der in the mid-dle of the field, An - gel work-ing at the char - i - ot wheel, Ain't so par -tic'- lar 'bout work-ing at the wheel, But I

just want to see how the char - iot feels. Oh, let me fly, ___

Guitar   Let me fly, ___

Guitar - play either high or low part

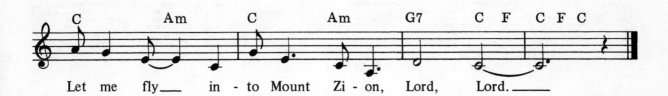

Let me fly___ in - to Mount Zi - on, Lord, Lord. ___

CF   C   F   C F   C F
I got a mother in the Promised Land,
C   F   C F C F C F
Ain't gonna stop till I shake her hand.
C F   C   F   C   FC
Not so partic'lar 'bout shaking her hand,
F   C   F   CF   C F   C F
But I just want to go to the Promised Land.
      Chorus

  C F C   F C F C   F
Meet that hypocrite on the street,
  C   F   C F   C F C F
First thing he'll do is to show his teeth.
  C F   C F C FC
Next thing he'll do is to tell a lie,
  F   C   F   C F   C F C F
And the best thing to do is to pass him by.
      Chorus

181

The Three-Quarter Church Lick

- Finger a C chord.
- Play the bass, down-up church lick.
- Play another down-up.

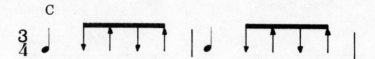

You can add a hammer-on in alternate measures when you have more than one consecutive measure of the same chord.

Add bass runs where you think they will fit.

Little Moses

A - way by the riv - er, so clear, ___ The la - dies were

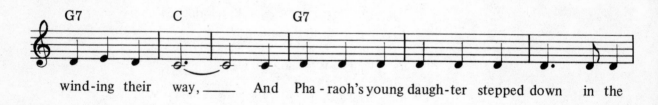

wind-ing their way, ___ And Pha - raoh's young daugh-ter stepped down in the

wa - ter to bathe in the cool of the day. ___ Be -

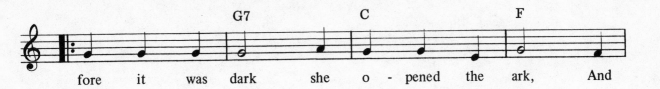

fore   it   was   dark   she   o - pened   the   ark,   And

found   the   sweet   in - fant   was   there._____   Be - ——

     C   G7   C
Away by the waters so blue,
            G7   C
The infant was lonely and sad.
  G7
She took him in pity and thought him so pretty,
    C   G7   C
And made little Moses so glad.
           G7   C   F
  She called him her own, her beautiful son,
    C   G7   C
And sent for a nurse that was near.
Repeat last two lines.

      C   G7 C
Away by the river so clear,
            G7   C
They carried the beautiful child,
  G7
To his tender mother, his sister and brother,
      C   G7   C
And Moses looked happy and smiled.
           G7   C   F
  His mother, so good, did all that she could
    C   G7   C
To rear him and teach him with care.
Repeat last two lines.

    C   G7   C
Away by the sea that was red,
             G7   C
Little Moses, the servant of God,
          G7
While in Him confided, the sea was divided,
    C   G7   C
As upward he lifted his rod.
                G7   C
  The Jews safely crossed, while King
          F
  Pharaoh's host
     C   G7   C
Was drowned in the waters and lost.
Repeat last two lines.

    C   G7   C
Away on a mountain so high,
             G7   C
The last one that ever might see.
  G7
While in him victorious, his hope was most
    glorious,
    C   G7   C
He'd soon over Jordan be free.
               G7   C
When his labors did cease, he left there
      F
  in peace,
     C   G7   C
And rested in heaven above.
Repeat last two lines.

183

Farther Along

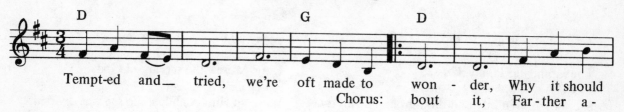

Tempt-ed and__ tried, we're oft made to wwon - der, Why it should
Chorus: bout it, Far - ther a -

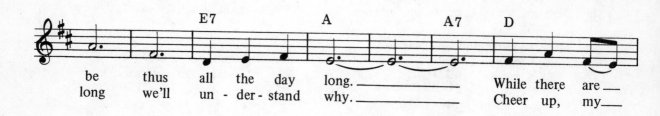

be thus all the day long. _____ While there are __
long we'll un - der - stand why. _____ Cheer up, my__

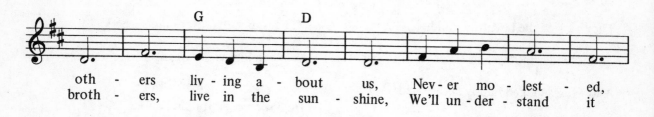

oth - ers liv - ing a - bout us, Nev - er mo - lest - ed,
broth - ers, live in the sun - shine, We'll un - der - stand it

Fine Chorus:

To chorus at measure 5

Though in the wrong. __ Far - ther a - long we'll know all a -
all by and by.

184

```
    D                    G        D
When death has come and taken our loved ones,
                         E7       A    A7
Leaving our homes so lone and so drear;
    D                    G        D
Then do we wonder why others prosper,
                    A7        D
Living as sinners, year after year. Chorus


    D              G     D
Often I wonder why I must journey
                   E7      A    A7
Over a road so rugged and steep;
    D                    G        D
While there are others living in comfort,
                    A7        D
While with the lost I labor and weep. Chorus


    D                      G        D
"Faithful till death," said our loving Master.
                   E7        A   A7
Only a while to labor and wait;
    D                 G     D
All of our toils will soon be forgotten,
                         A7        D
When we sweep through the beautiful gate. Chorus


    D                       G     D
Soon with the Lord, our wonderful Savior,
                     E7        A    A7
We'll be at home beyond the blue sky;
    D                   G          D
There we shall meet the dear ones a-waiting,
                A7        D
We'll understand it all by and by. Chorus
```

- Finger an E minor chord.
- Brush down with the thumb.

- Brush up with the first finger.
- Repeat over and over in the rocking rhythm.

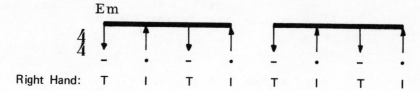

Keep Your Lamp Trimmed and Burning

Chorus:

Keep your lamp trimmed and a-burn-ing, Keep your lamp trimmed and burn-ing,

Fine

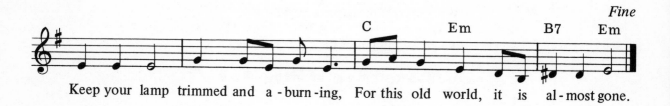

Keep your lamp trimmed and a-burn-ing, For this old world, it is al-most gone.

Verse:

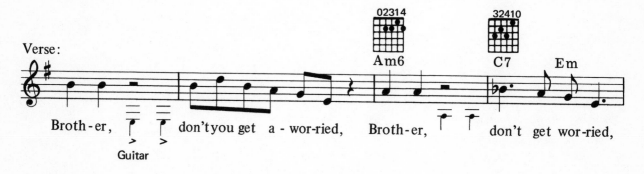

Broth-er, don't you get a-wor-ried, Broth-er, don't get wor-ried,

Guitar

G   B7 B7 E7   A7   C   Em   B7   Em

Broth-er,   don't get a-wor-ried,_ For this old world, it is al-most done.

    Em
Sister, don't you stop a-praying,
Am6 C7   Em
Sister, don't stop praying,
 G B7 B7 E7   A7
Sister,   don't stop a-praying,
  C   Em   B7 Em
For this old world, it is almost done. *Chorus*

    Em
Preacher, don't you stop a-preaching,
  Am6   C7   Em
Preacher, don't stop preaching,
  G   B7 B7 E7   A7
Preacher,   don't stop a-preaching,
  C   Em   B7 Em
For this old world, it is almost done. *Chorus*

Can you make up some verses of your own?

The Rocking Arpeggio

- Finger an A minor chord.

- In your good old rocking rhythm play the following arpeggio.

Right hand: T 1 3 1 T 1 3 1 T 1 3 1 T 1 3 1

2 2 2 2

together

This arpeggio is to be used in the chorus of *Wade in the Water*. Watch out for the changing bass notes of the A minor chords.

For the verse, play one beat per chord. That beat may be played either by a light thumb-brush downward or a thumb-fingers pluck.

Avoid striking the x-marked strings on some of the chords by having your thumb "leap" over them quickly.

Enjoy the sound of these "new" chords. Enjoy . . .

Wade in the Water

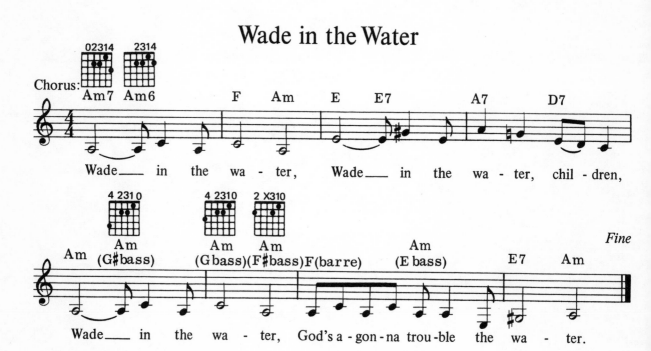

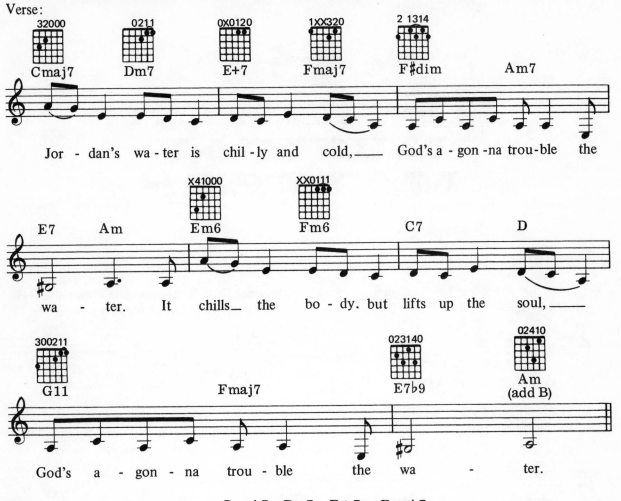

Verse:

Cmaj7 (32000) Dm7 (0211) E+7 (0X0120) Fmaj7 (1XX320) F#dim (2 1314) Am7

Jor - dan's wa - ter is chil - ly and cold,___ God's a - gon -na trou -ble the

E7 Am Em6 (X41000) Fm6 (XX0111) C7 D

wa - ter. It chills_ the bo - dy. but lifts up the soul, ___

G11 (300211) Fmaj7 E7b9 (023140) Am (add B) (02410)

God's a - gon - na trou - ble the wa - ter.

C maj 7   Dm7   E+7   F maj 7
Jordan's water is deep and wide,
  F# dim   Am7   E7 Am
  God's a-gonna trouble the wa–ter.
Em6   Fm6   C7   D
Meet my mother on the other side,
  G11   F maj 7 E7b9 Am (add B)
  God's a-gonna trouble the wa – ter.
      Chorus

C maj 7   Dm7   E+7 F maj 7
If you get there before I do.
  F# dim   Am7   E7 Am
  God's a-gonna trouble the wa–ter.
    Em6   Fm6   C7   D
Tell all of my friends I'm coming, too,
  G11   F maj 7 E7b9 Am (add B)
  God's a-gonna trouble the wa – ter.
      Chorus

189

6
REVIEWING MUSICAL MATTERS

Note-Reading Review

Since the notes we have learned to read have been scattered throughout the pages of this book, here is the complete **chromatic scale** up to the twelfth fret of the first string.

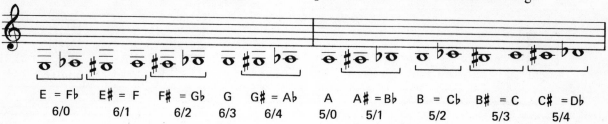

E = F♭	E♯ = F	F♯ = G♭	G	G♯ = A♭	A	A♯ = B♭	B = C♭	B♯ = C	C♯ = D♭
6/0	6/1	6/2	6/3	6/4	5/0	5/1	5/2	5/3	5/4

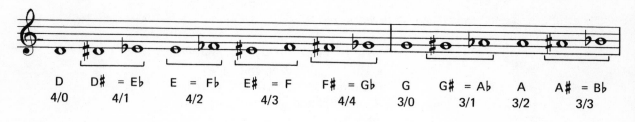

D	D♯ = E♭	E = F♭	E♯ = F	F♯ = G♭	G	G♯ = A♭	A	A♯ = B♭
4/0	4/1	4/2	4/3	4/4	3/0	3/1	3/2	3/3

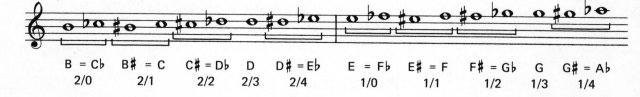

B = C♭	B♯ = C	C♯ = D♭	D	D♯ = E♭	E = F♭	E♯ = F	F♯ = G♭	G	G♯ = A♭
2/0	2/1	2/2	2/3	2/4	1/0	1/1	1/2	1/3	1/4

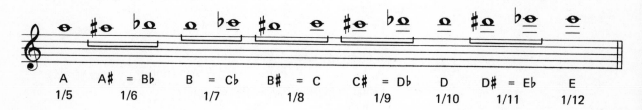

A	A♯ = B♭	B = C♭	B♯ = C	C♯ = D♭	D	D♯ = E♭	E
1/5	1/6	1/7	1/8	1/9	1/10	1/11	1/12

190

Note Value and Timing Review

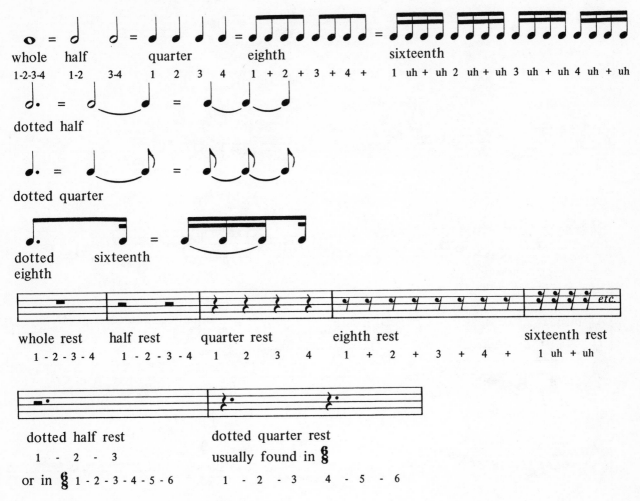

Key Signature and Scale Review

We have worked with five major keys and some of their relative minors. Here are those keys as well as all the remaining keys we have not studied.

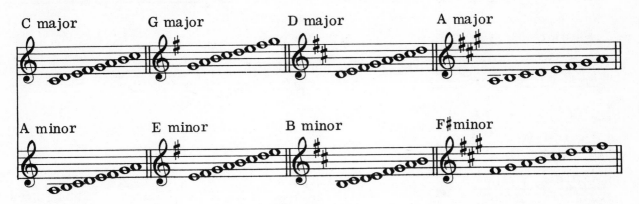

192

Transposing Review

We are now in a position to develop a more complete chord transposing table than was presented at the end of Chapter One. The types of chords (major, minor, diminished, etc.) are not differentiated here. What we are concerned with is the "spelling." For keys other than those given here consult the above scales.

CHORDS

KEY	I	II	III	IV	V	VI	VII
C	C	D	E	F	G	A	B
G	G	A	B	C	D	E	F♯
D	D	E	F♯	G	A	B	C♯
A	A	B	C♯	D	E	F♯	G♯
E	E	F♯	G♯	A	B	C♯	D♯
Am	A	B	C	D	E	F	G
Em	E	F♯	G	A	B	C	D
Dm	D	E	F	G	A	B♭	C

Tuning the Guitar

Tuning any musical instrument accurately is a technical matter which depends not so much on one's ability to play that instrument but rather on the sensitivity and musical receptivity of one's ear. With a stringed instrument like a guitar, tuning is a constant "problem." The guitar may go out of tune at any time— between playings or, indeed, while playing. The ability to get it back in tune (after first recognizing that it is out of tune) is very difficult to teach because it involves that very elusive faculty, hearing.

Nevertheless, there are certain mechanical devices you can use to get your instrument back in tune, provided you know what to listen for.

Tuning to a Piano

Here are the notes on the piano which correspond to the six open strings of the guitar.

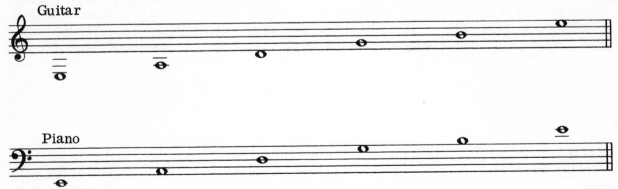

You may notice that the piano notes seem to be written an octave lower than the corresponding guitar notes. Actually, by long-standing tradition, it is the guitar notes which are written one octave higher than they actually sound. Another way of saying this is: The guitar sounds one octave lower than written.

As you play and compare piano note to guitar string, you have to make the judgment: Is the guitar higher, lower or the same as the piano?

- If it is *higher,* turn the tuning peg slowly in the *loosening* direction. Keep playing the string as you tune. Keep comparing it with the piano. When the two notes are in tune go on to the next string.

- If it is *lower,* turn the peg slowly in the *tightening* direction and proceed as above.

Tuning to a Pitchpipe

A **pitchpipe** is a whistle (or a set of six whistles) tuned to one or more notes of the scale. You make the same comparisons and judgments with the pitchpipe as you do with the piano. It may help if you sing the note sounded by the pitchpipe and also the note of the guitar.

Tuning Relative to Itself

If no pianos or pitchpipes are available it is still possible to tune the guitar *relative to itself.* This requires a certain amount of experience since there is no standard pitch to which to compare your guitar. You simply have to get the "feel" of what a reasonably in-tune sixth string sounds like and take it from there.

This method of tuning uses the principle that the note of each open string is also playable on the string immediately lower than it (except, of course, for the sixth string).

This is how it works:

- Having made your commitment to the "in-tuneness" of the E (sixth string) by tightening, loosening or leaving it alone, play the tone at the *fifth fret* of the sixth string. This is A, the note that should sound on the open fifth string.

- Play the fifth string. Make the comparison between its A and that sounding on the fifth fret of the sixth string. Tune accordingly.

- After you are satisfied that the fifth and sixth strings are in tune, play the *fifth fret* of the fifth string. This gives you D, the note of the fourth open string. Tune the fourth string.

- The *fifth fret* of the fourth string gives you G, the note you wish to match on the third open string.

- The *fourth fret* of the third string gives you the B you desire as the note of the second open string.

- The *fifth fret* of the second string gives you E, the note of the first open string.

Theoretically, you are now in tune. Actually, some adjustments may have to be made. Repeat the whole process as many times as necessary in order to refine the inevitable errors and get the strings as closely in tune with each other as possible. If you play some six-string chords—E minor is a good one—you may be able to hear which strings are not quite in tune.

CHORD CHART

The following symbols are used in this chart:

P = Primary bass string   o = Open string to be played

A = Alternate bass string   x = String not to be played

▬▬▬ = Barre

The number to the right of some of the diagrams indicates the fret.

Some of the fingerings presented here may differ from the way they appeared in the text. Both are correct.

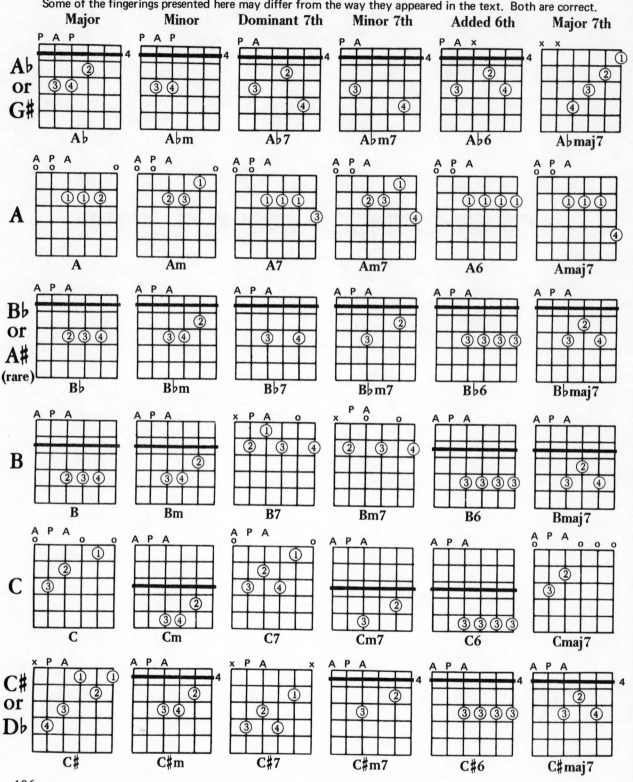

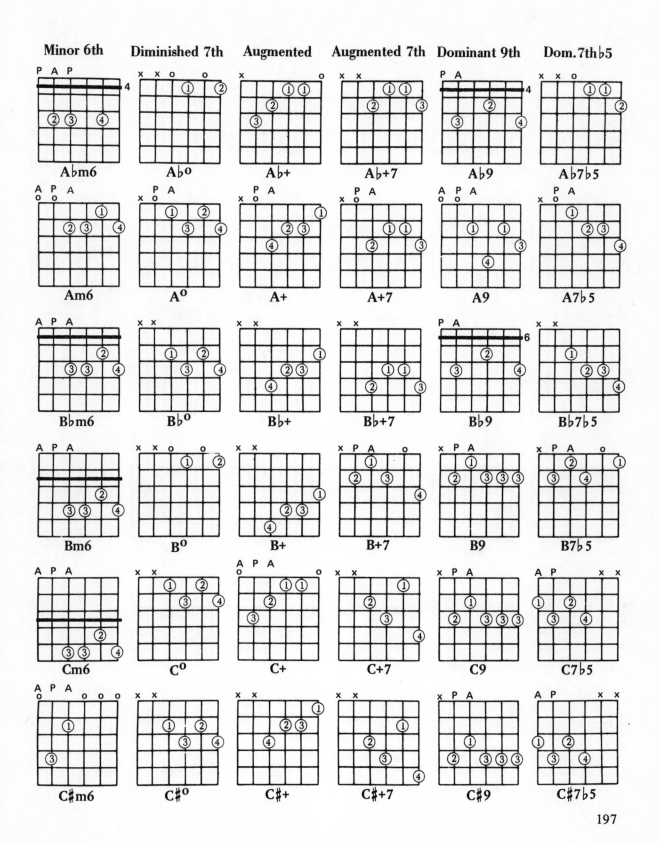

Minor 6th | Diminished 7th | Augmented | Augmented 7th | Dominant 9th | Dom. 7th♭5

Abm6 | Ab° | Ab+ | Ab+7 | Ab9 | Ab7♭5

Am6 | A° | A+ | A+7 | A9 | A7♭5

Bbm6 | Bb° | Bb+ | Bb+7 | Bb9 | Bb7♭5

Bm6 | B° | B+ | B+7 | B9 | B7♭5

Cm6 | C° | C+ | C+7 | C9 | C7♭5

C#m6 | C#° | C#+ | C#+7 | C#9 | C#7♭5

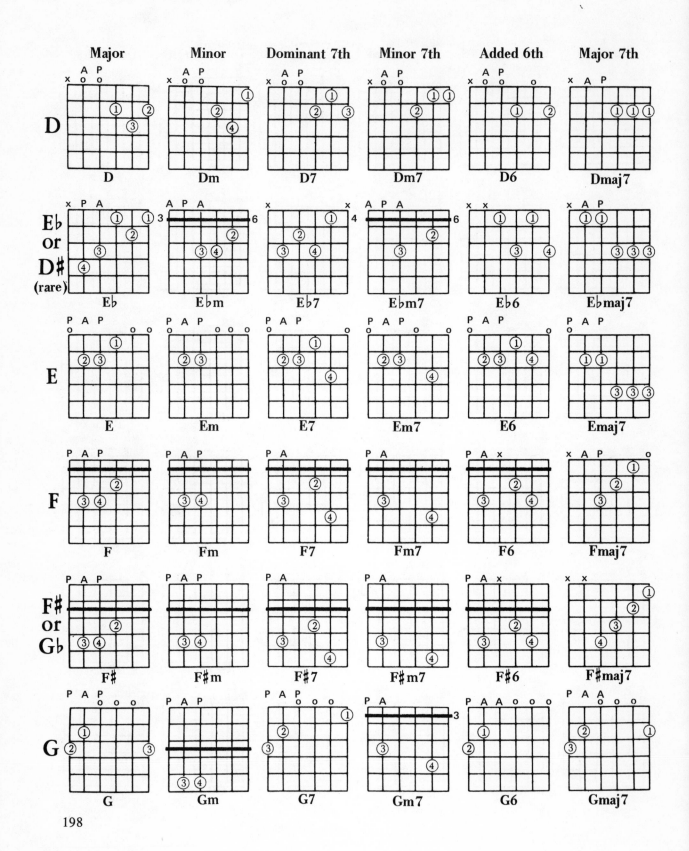

Minor 6th	Diminished 7th	Augmented	Augmented 7th	Dominant 9th	Dom. 7th♭5

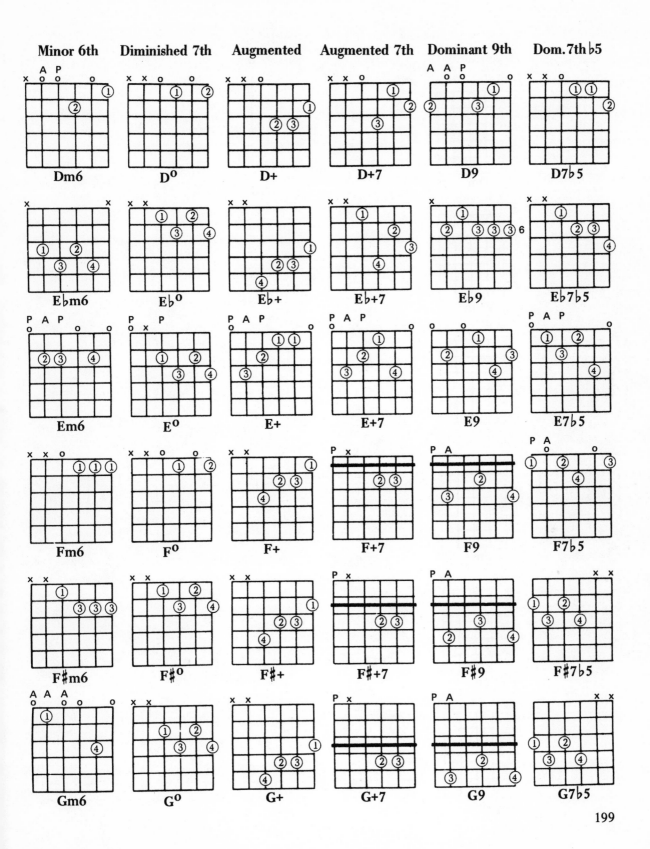

Dm6 · D° · D+ · D+7 · D9 · D7♭5

E♭m6 · E♭° · E♭+ · E♭+7 · E♭9 · E♭7♭5

Em6 · E° · E+ · E+7 · E9 · E7♭5

Fm6 · F° · F+ · F+7 · F9 · F7♭5

F♯m6 · F♯° · F♯+ · F♯+7 · F♯9 · F♯7♭5

Gm6 · G° · G+ · G+7 · G9 · G7♭5